The Power of Middle School

Other Titles of Interest by
Rowman & Littlefield Education

The Middle School Mind: Growing Pains in Early Adolescent Brains, by Richard M. Marshall and Sharon Neuman

Learn to Think and Write: A Paradigm for Teaching Grades 4–8, Introductory Levels, by Una McGinley Sarno

Learn to Think and Write: A Paradigm for Teaching Grades 4–8, Advanced Levels, by Una McGinley Sarno

Surviving the Move and Learning to Thrive: Tools for Success in Secondary Schools, by Lisa Anne Fisher

Teaching Middle School Language Arts: Incorporating Twenty-First Century Literacies, by Anna J. Small

Cultural Journeys: Multicultural Literature for Elementary and Middle School Students, by Pamela S. Gates and Dianne L. Hall Mark

Off the Bus! How Teachers Can Help Students and Parents Transition to Middle School, by Mary Ann Smialek

The Power of Middle School

Maximizing These Vital Years

Keen Babbage

ROWMAN & LITTLEFIELD EDUCATION
A division of
ROWMAN & LITTLEFIELD PUBLISHERS, INC.
Lanham • New York • Toronto • Plymouth, UK

Published by Rowman & Littlefield Education
A division of Rowman & Littlefield Publishers, Inc.
A wholly owned subsidiary of The Rowman & Littlefield Publishing Group, Inc.
4501 Forbes Boulevard, Suite 200, Lanham, Maryland 20706
www.rowman.com

10 Thornbury Road, Plymouth PL6 7PP, United Kingdom

British Library Cataloguing in Publication Information Available

Library of Congress Cataloging-in-Publication Data

Babbage, Keen J.
The power of middle school : maximizing these vital years / Keen Babbage.
p. cm.
ISBN 978-1-61048-702-3 (cloth : alk. paper) -- ISBN 978-1-61048-703-0 (pbk. : alk. paper) -- ISBN 978-1-61048-704-7 (electronic) 1. Middle school education--United States. 2. Middle schools--United States. 3. Middle school teachers--Training of--United States. 4. School improvement programs--United States. I. Title.
LB1623.5.B34 2012
373.236--dc23
2012020132

Printed in the United States of America

To my parents, Bob and Judy Babbage, and to my grandparents, Keen and Eunice Johnson. Those saints are responsible for everything good in life that I have experienced or accomplished.

Contents

Preface

"What happened to my son?" "What happened to my daughter?" During my thirteen years as a middle school administrator those questions or similar questions were heard each year. Parents and guardians were sincerely seeking answers as they saw unexpected, unprecedented, and complex changes occur in their children aged eleven to fourteen.

The answer for those parents and guardians should not be a generic statement of, "Oh, it will work out. These things happen in the years between elementary school and high school. Your child will be fine once all of the changes and the extremes of the middle school years settle down."

The answer for those parents and guardians who may be experiencing middle school for the first time or, if having experienced middle school with an older child are now having a somewhat different experience with their child who is in middle school now, can be very clear, direct, and personal.

That is a very important question. I have talked to your son several times. Thomas is always very polite with me. He sure loves soccer. He gives me a soccer report every Monday at lunch so I know about his weekend game. I visit classes often so I see him in class. He seems to behave well and pay attention, but his grades this year are declining. He made the Honor Roll as a 6th grader. He is making C grades now and some D grades.

He did get in trouble in the cafeteria last week when he threw a french fry at a student he used to be friends with, but they had some disagreement that day. His teachers tell me that this year Thomas seems eager to show off in class sometimes. Maybe there is another student he is trying to impress.

I think we can get this turned around. This school has excellent guidance counselors. Thomas's teachers meet daily as a teaching team so you can talk with all of them. There are several actions we can consider to add more structure to what Thomas does at school. Here's one possibility. For the next two weeks, have Thomas see me as soon as he arrives at school. Let's begin each day with that conversation. After he sees me, he will check with the teacher who is his team leader so they can review his homework and solve any problem that has come up. The guidance counselor who works with Thomas will meet with you and Thomas's teachers to identify what else needs to be done. Thomas can attend part of the meeting.

Our school is very serious about building wholesome relationships between students, families, teachers, counselors, staff, and administrators. We are also very serious about being flexible and creative enough to solve problems individually. If everyone, Thomas included, works together we should get good results.

As far as what happened to Thomas is concerned, he is a 7th grader and he may think that since the 6th graders are younger, he has some new rank or seniority. There may be a girl he likes. I notice a growth spurt in Thomas. A lot happens during these amazing middle school years. We will get through this together and our goals will be for Thomas to return to the Honor Roll plus to get back on the straight and narrow. Still, the middle school path sometimes has detours. He is on a detour now. We can resolve this.

If the middle school years are maximized the results can be outstanding. These years are filled with potential, promise, problems, and possibilities. For current and future educational achievement, these years are vital. In some ways, the good work that can be done in middle school cannot be done as effectively or as efficiently at any other time. This book is about ways to maximize the vital middle school years.

Names and characters presented in this book are fictional. The situations, the ideas, the insights, and the opportunities presented in this book are real. Let's explore the amazing, vital middle school years with the intentions of maximizing the productivity, progress, and achievements of students and maximizing the meaningful career experiences of middle school educators while also providing guidance to families of middle school students.

Acknowledgments

From 1984 to 1988 I taught 7th and 8th graders at the Beechwood Independent School District in Fort Mitchell, Kentucky. With those students I learned how fascinating and meaningful the middle school experience could be for students and for teachers.

From 1993 to 2006 I was the assistant principal of Bryan Station Middle School in Lexington, Kentucky. The dedicated faculty and staff daily showed what middle school could mean to and provide for students. During some of those years I also got to teach 7th and 8th grade elective classes. The students eagerly learned and their teacher learned also.

Jim Thomas served as principal of Bryan Station Middle School in Lexington for many years. His leadership was exemplary. His knowledge of and his devotion to middle school are vast. His guidance on this book was vital.

During 1966 to 1969 I was a student at Morton Junior High, now middle school, in Lexington, Kentucky. Our teachers were serious, demanding, and caring. The wisdom they shared continues to benefit many people.

From 2006 to 2012 I have taught U.S. history and political science at Henry Clay High School in Lexington, Kentucky. Some of the students I have taught had been students at the middle school where I was the assistant principal. Working with those students for seven consecutive years of middle school and high school was especially rewarding and revealing. Insights from those experiences confirmed for me the importance of maximizing the vital years of middle school.

Keen J. Babbage
Lexington, Kentucky
April 2012

Chapter One

The Unique Possibilities of Middle School

How should the term "middle school" be defined? "It's the school for students who have completed elementary school." "It is the school for students who are not yet old enough for high school." Those statements are true, but they address only chronology. Middle school is not merely the step between elementary school and high school. The middle school years are not merely the step between almost-a-teenager and initially-becoming-a-teenager. What, then, vividly describes or defines middle school?

The more foundational question could be "Is middle school—a separate, uniquely designed educational facility and program for students aged eleven to fourteen—necessary?" Could elementary school be extended and advanced to include all grades from kindergarten until high school? Are nine years of schooling, kindergarten through 8th grade, needed prior to starting high school? Was the old junior high school approach sufficient or is an educational program for eleven- to fourteen-year-olds better if it seeks to accomplish goals that include preparation for high school and more immediate objectives?

For our purposes, the need for middle school has proven itself. The eleven- to fourteen-year-olds are not the youngest children and are not the oldest teenagers, yet much more than age determines the importance of a separate school and the need for a separate school.

There are academic, personal, interpersonal, achievement, accomplishment, developmental, and social steps that students aged eleven to fourteen are ready for and need to master. It is the comprehensive academic, exploratory, supportive, mentoring, extracurricular program of a middle school combined with a personal organizational structure that can effectively educate

1

students who have completed an elementary school program, yet need to master a new set of experiences to complete their preparation for high school and for their older teenage years.

We return to an earlier question: What vividly describes or defines middle school? Shawn describes middle school or maybe middle school describes Shawn. Tasha defines middle school or perhaps middle school defines Tasha. Knowing Shawn and Tasha will provide an authentic description of and definition of middle school.

Shawn is in the 6th grade. He would be glad to tell you about himself.

My name is Shawn Barrett. I am eleven years old, but I'll be twelve next month. I'm in the 6th grade at Memorial Middle School. We went back to school a few weeks ago in August. I don't really like school, but I don't really hate school. Well, I do like my technology education class because I'm pretty good with computers. And I like my math class because it's not like most math classes. The teacher makes us work a lot, but, you know, we do neat stuff.

I mean, in most classes we do the same stuff we did in 5th grade. The teachers said we had to review for a month or two. The math teacher said we had to get ready for the football season, the end of the baseball season, the election in November, and then the holidays. We do all kinds of math problems about sports and voters and holiday shopping. It's pretty cool.

I see my friends at school and we have fun together. Thomas used to be my best friend, but not any more. He started some rumor about me and I got really mad. I got in trouble for yelling at him during my English class. It was all sort of stupid. My kind-of friend Alex told me that Thomas told him that I like Allison. She's nice, but I really liked Katy and when Katy heard I like Allison, well, everything got crazy.

Thomas, Alex, Allison, and Katy plus me, we had to meet with a school counselor and with the assistant principal. Nobody got in trouble except me. I was so dumb to believe what Alex said. He set the whole thing up to make me get mad at Thomas. Well, Alex sure isn't my friend anymore and Thomas and I, well, we're almost friends again. Katy and Allison never get in any trouble but they'll be mad at me forever.

I'm in the school band, but I don't like it. When I was in the 4th grade I wanted to play trumpet like my big sister did. She's in high school now and she's in the marching band. So I wanted to be like her because she loved band in middle school. She was in 8th grade when I was in 4th grade and I really wanted to be in the band just like my big sister.

Now my parents make me take band because they paid for some trumpet lessons I took. They said it was my idea to play trumpet and I have to keep doing it until 9th grade. Then I can decide on my own what to do. I already know I'll quit. When I'm in high school I want to play soccer. My middle school has a soccer team, but the coach is my science teacher and he doesn't like me. So I don't want to be on his team.

I know he doesn't like me because he gives me bad grades no matter what I do. He calls on me when I don't know the answer and he never calls on me when I do know the answer. That's not all. I sit next to Katy in that class. I asked the teacher to move me. He said no. He let another student move, but not me. That's not fair. Maybe we'll have a new soccer coach next year.

Oh, yeah, you probably want to know about my grades. They're not bad. I never make F or D grades. I make a few A's, but mostly B's. My big sister is brilliant and my brother is a genius. He's in 8th grade at the same school I go to. Some teachers asked me if I am as smart as my brother. What kind of question is that? He's super smart. I'm pretty smart. Isn't pretty smart good enough?

Well, that's about it. One more thing. I got a dog when I was four years old. Buster is his name. He's almost eight years old, but he's getting sick a lot. Buster really is my best friend. He gets so excited when I come home from school, but he just can't play like he used to. I don't know what will happen to him. I kind of worry about that. I hope he gets better. He's been with me forever. Things just wouldn't be right without Buster. It's something I think about sometimes, well, a lot of times.

* * *

Hi, I'm Tasha. Tasha Kimberly Hart. I'm in the 7th grade at Memorial Middle School. I'm involved in everything. I've always been involved in everything, well, not the dance team and not sports, but most everything else. And I always know what is going on at school. I know who likes who. I know who just broke up. I know the latest news. And I also make good grades plus I stay out of trouble. How do I do all of that? It's easy. Here's what I do.

I do my homework right after I get home. Actually, I get most of it done at school. A lot of my teachers give us some time in class to get started on our homework. They say it lets them be sure we get started right. Well, the homework is usually really easy. Some worksheet or other stuff like that. Whatever I don't finish at school I do at home right after I get home. My parents never have to ask about my homework. When they get home from work, my homework is finished.

Then I have chores to do. I walk the dog. I empty trash cans. I clean my room. I even help with laundry. It's easy stuff, but I learned last year when I complained about chores that complaining makes it worse. I never had to do the laundry until I complained about emptying the trash cans. For each complaint I would get a new chore. That just happened once.

So, I really like to walk my dog. Her name is Kim, which comes from my middle name. I really wanted a dog when I was little. On my sixth birthday I got a dog so it just seemed right, you know, to name the dog after me.

So, why do I like to walk the dog? Well, she's really fun to be with. She's always glad to see me and she loves to walk. That's not all. My really good friend, Rachel, she lives in my neighborhood and she has a dog. So we call each other almost every day after we get home from school and we make plans to walk our dogs together. Rachel and I get to talk about everything while we walk the dogs.

Yesterday Rachel told me that she heard that Tommy, he's this really cute 8th grader at our school, well, she said that Tommy likes me. I was sort of excited, but, well, I mean, I used to like Tommy last year, but he never paid any attention to me because I was just a 6th grader then.

I'm not so sure about Tommy. I heard from my best friend Olivia at school today that Tommy really likes this other girl named Candace, but he got the rumor started that he likes me so Candace would get jealous. It's pretty stupid. Tommy is cute, but he's not that cute. Sometimes boys just cause problems and Tommy, well, he just seems like trouble to me. He's not cute enough to get in some dumb rumor war over.

So I'm involved in lots of stuff. I like to sing. We have this really great choir at school. It's a class every day and it's a club that meets after school sometimes. We have concerts and we have guest singers who meet with us and show us about singing. They come from a college that's close to our school. It's pretty neat.

I'd love to sing, you know, really sing like famous singers. I'd like to take some extra lessons. My parents said they would pay half of that. So I have to babysit or something to make my half. I could probably do that, but if I worked that hard for the money I'd rather buy some new clothes. I don't know. Maybe one of those college people could give me lessons for a lower price.

Anyway, I sing in the youth choir at church. I go with my parents once a month to volunteer at a food bank. I am in lots of clubs at school. I help with the school yearbook and with the morning announcements on the TV system at school. I get to school early once a week to help tutor 6th graders in math. Some of those little 6th graders are really lost. I wonder if I was like that last year. I mean they are still trying to find their way around the school and unlock their locker and stuff like that.

One other thing. I make really good grades. I mean Honor Roll all the time. It's not hard. I don't see how some students get in trouble with bad grades. I think middle school is easier than elementary school. Almost all we have to do is read chapters and answer questions or do worksheets. It's easy. Homework is usually just another chapter or another worksheet. It's so easy. The students who do nothing are strange. I never really talk to them because, well, it sounds mean, but I don't like them and I don't want to be like them.

I know one girl who had to repeat 6th grade. She's a 6th grader again this year. She never did any work last year. We were friends in elementary school, but she got kind of strange last year. Something must have happened. I heard that her parents got divorced, but when I asked her last year she said no. Actually she yelled no and told me to leave her alone. So I just leave her alone. I hope she does better this year. We were pretty good friends back in 5th grade. Maybe I should talk to her. Maybe I could tutor her in math. But she's smart. I wonder why she failed 6th grade.

A group of very accomplished and very respected past and present middle school teachers, counselors, and administrators were asked via a written qualitative survey to provide perspectives to be used in this book. The first question on the survey helps us know more about Tasha, Shawn, and other middle school students. The question was "What is the most unique charac-teristic of middle school students?" The insights from survey participants follow:

- "Developing a sense of identity."
- "Middle school students can be a child one moment and then turn around to be a teenager the next moment."
- "The most unique characteristic of middle school students is their never-ending energy."
- "Just as they think they have things figured out, they have another dose of hormones hit them and they are right back at square one."
- "The students are all different. Different stages of development; different sizes physically; different levels of maturity. They range from 'babies' to almost grown."
- "Middle school students are experiencing dramatic changes in physical development at various rates. They tend to be very sensitive and have a strong need for approval from others. Peers begin to have a greater influ-ence during the middle school years."
- "Their moods. They can be 'up' one hour and 'down' the next. Fitting in is everything to them. Both boys and girls constantly seek to fit in."
- "They grow and change on a day-to-day basis more than any other group."
- "Most middle school students have incredible emotional ties to learning."
- "Middle school students are so indecisive. One minute they want us to hold their hands and the next minute the students think they are the adults."
- "The individual quirkiness they have. Hormones are raging. They have one foot in childhood and one foot in young adulthood. They are trying to figure out who they are and where they belong."
- "Unpredictable mood swings. Also, the uncertainty as they realize they don't spend all day with one teacher."

We have met Tasha and Shawn, both of whom are middle school students. It is important to avoid describing Tasha and Shawn as typical middle school students because although eleven- to fourteen-year-olds do share several characteristics, each student has a unique set of life experiences, a unique personality, and unique degrees of development in many areas.

It is true that middle school students tend to share several or many com-mon characteristics. It is also true that no two middle school students are exactly alike. Much is revealed through an awareness of the common charac-teristics. Those commonly held characteristics help shape the beginning real-ity of a middle school. What middle school educators do in response to those commonly held characteristics of middle school students can help direct the success or failure of the school.

Is the definition of a middle school elusive? Can tendencies, likely characteristics, and commonalities among middle school students combined with proper educational objectives for eleven- to fourteen-year-olds provide sufficient guidance toward a middle school definition?

Let's try to define middle school, but in attempting this we are reminded that by its very nature, a middle school can be a dynamic, lively, changing atmosphere as it reflects and educates the dynamic, lively, changing students. In many ways, middle school is a bridge. The middle school bridge goes from childhood on one side to adolescence on the other side, from almost a teenager on one side to beginning the teenage years on the other side, from completion of elementary school on one side to ready for high school on the other side, from questions about "who I am" on one side to more awareness of "who I am" on the other side, from a new academic beginning on one side to new academic development on the other side.

Yet this middle school bridge is unlike any bridge on a highway or on a road. Transportation bridges are usually a straight line from point A to point B. Transportation bridges may have some minor amount of elevation, but they generally appear to be flat or close to flat. A driver does not expect a bridge going across a river to be filled with turns or twists, steep elevation or sharp descents, barriers or blockades. The driver on a transportation bridge does not expect signs that communicate "stop," "reduce speed," "change lanes," "danger ahead," "turn around," or "alternate route ahead."

The middle school bridge is designed like a maze. There is an entrance and there is an exit; however, the journey between the entrance and the exit is not perfectly straight and is not perfectly flat. Some sections of the maze are steep, some sections are flat, and some sections descend. Some sections are quiet and others are very noisy. Some wide parts allow swift passage and other parts are very narrow, requiring slow, cautious, careful steps. Sometimes the traffic flows with you in a one-way passage while other portions have multiple directions with various options, some of which lead toward the exit while others lead away from the exit.

The middle school maze does have many official signs that provide beneficial directions. When these directions are followed the journey is still not simple, but it is simpler than if those helpful directions are disobeyed or are ignored. The middle school maze has some unofficial signs or communications that lead to mistaken detours that can keep a traveler perpetually returning toward the entrance rather than making steady or fairly steady progress toward the exit.

As a middle school student goes through grades 6, 7, and 8 there are challenges, opportunities, trials, errors, successes, achievements, changes, certainties, questions, answers, pressures, standards, virtues and vices, learning experiences that teach the curriculum, and other possible experiences which ideally are avoided but can realistically occur.

Some middle school students travel through the maze efficiently while others confront many complications. Most middle school students find the maze presents, at least, an occasional challenge, while for other students, the maze seems to be a constant challenge.

As the middle school student lives his or her years from eleven years old to twelve, thirteen, and fourteen, thoughts, feelings, ideas, emotions, bodies, minds, hearts, friendships, interests, goals, hobbies, ambitions, and behaviors can be dynamic unlike any other segment within the scope of human growth and development during the years of kindergarten through high school.

All of this middle school reality, possibility, opportunity, responsibility, adventure, and challenge face each middle school student, parent/guardian, teacher, counselor, administrator, and staff member daily. For some educators, the uniqueness of middle school students and the importance of maximizing the school results that are possible during these vital years are some of the reasons to work in middle school throughout a career. It is their duty, their calling, their passion, their joy, their service, and the career that they chose and that reciprocally chose them.

For other educators, working at middle school is to be avoided because there is a better match elsewhere. Everyone benefits when the match is correct. Approach middle school knowing how wonderful the match can be, yet knowing that a mismatch is miserable.

For students, the middle school maze need not have any permanent obstacles; however, it does have challenging choices and difficult decisions, yet it also has opportunities for bold discoveries and meaningful achievements. The middle school maze can be navigated with minimal setbacks and limited errors, but not without some moments of perplexity, confusion, or uncertainty.

As middle school educators create purposefully designed learning experiences, character building experiences, mentoring guidance, and partnerships with parents/guardians, the middle school years become a time when the maze is a meaningful challenge and a rewarding adventure with mostly steady progress despite some occasional setbacks or unproductive detours.

The a-maze-ing middle school years present the eleven-, twelve-, thirteen-, and fourteen-year-olds with adventures, challenges, complexities, successes, failures, joys, trials, errors, learning, obedience, disobedience, and a way to make vital progress toward essential goals. Life and school are not suddenly cruel and unfair, placing middle school students in a trap, a box, or a cage.

No, it is a maze filled with decisions that can be made correctly, turns or intersections that can be traveled wisely, and setbacks that can be fully overcome. The maze is middle school reality. Mastering the maze is the middle school duty, the middle school educators' responsibility, and the middle school students' unlimited opportunity.

The uniqueness of middle school students, as described by survey input shown earlier in this chapter and as applied in the middle school maze analogy, present to middle school educators some characteristics that are very education-friendly and that are conducive to very productive teaching.

Contrast the following two approaches for helping middle school students learn about the solar system in their 8th grade science class.

First Teacher: Good morning. We have a lot to cover today. You will have pages of notes to take. I will put some notes on the board as we go. Other notes will be from what I emphasize as I lecture. Everything today is about our solar system. You may have questions as we go, but save those for tomorrow because we need to cover all the planets and some other details today. So, listen closely. Pay attention. Keep up with the notes using the note format we always use. First, the planet that is closest to the sun is Mercury.

* * *

Second Teacher: Good morning. Today we begin studying the solar system. Yes, Allison. Do you have a question or an idea?

Allison: Last summer I went to this really neat museum that had a huge telescope. We could see all sorts of stuff in space. It was, like, so real and cool. Can we do something like that?

Second Teacher: [thinks for a moment] Of course. There are some really good Web sites that are showing what telescopes can see. I have a video about one museum like the place you visited. Then in a few days we'll turn the classroom into a solar system model with planets you'll make. So, yes, we can do a lot like that. Good idea, Allison.

Now, for today we have four different parts in class. First, we will organize ourselves into the solar system. Several of you will stand in the center of the classroom representing the sun. Others will represent each planet and move around the sun in your orbits. Others will represent various moons throughout the solar system and a few of you will represent spacecraft that are on their way to various planets.

Second, we have a short video that shows pictures of the moon and pictures of Mars. These are actual photographs from when astronauts went to the moon and from when a space vehicle roamed on Mars.

Third, we will each draw our version of a map of the solar system. We have lots of materials to use so everyone can draw their solar system map.

Fourth, we have a chart to analyze. The chart is filled with facts about the solar system, the sun, the planets, and our moon. We will create notes together based on our analysis of the facts in that chart. Now, let's start. When you came into class, I gave you a small card that told you which part of the solar system you would represent in the model we will make together. The five of you who are going to represent the sun need to move to the very center of the classroom where I have a yellow spot marked on the floor. Then we will add the rest of the solar system.

Which of these two lesson plans is more likely to get good results with 8th grade science students? Why will that lesson plan work better? What makes that lesson plan more likely to productively apply some of the unique characteristics of middle school students that can be incorporated into education-friendly teaching that causes learning? What is wrong with the other lesson plan, especially in what ways does it work against the realistic characteristics of middle school students, thus causing unnecessary problems for the teacher and for the students while also limiting what is learned?

We are told that middle school students are energetic, erratic, subject to mood changes, emotional, changing physically, exploring self-identity, unpredictable, and that no two middle school students are exactly alike. How productive will it be to tell an age group with such characteristics to sit down, be still, and be quiet for three years so they can listen to lectures, take notes, complete worksheets, and answer questions at the end of chapters?

How much more productive would it be to create learning experiences that are energetic, that include physical movement whenever possible, that include discovery rather than mere pedantic acquisition of static information, that invite curiosity, and that incorporate multiple activities?

There is a middle school curriculum that the students must master. The curriculum establishes what is to be learned. Unless restrictions are imposed, how that curriculum is taught and learned will and should vary. Just as no two middle school students are exactly alike, no two groups of middle school students are exactly alike, and no two consecutive classes of 7th graders are exactly alike.

The life experiences, the school experiences, the educational attainment, the personalities, the maturity level, personal discipline standards, and people skills of middle school students vary. The reality of middle school characteristics and the further reality that no two middle school students have the exact same mixture of those characteristics present middle school educators with an unlimited opportunity and adventure to create fascinating and effective learning experiences that apply rather than battle those genuine characteristics.

Yes, middle school students must be taught the desired behaviors that are required throughout the school and in each classroom. Yes, obedience to those required behaviors will increase when proper conduct is favorably acknowledged. Yes, disobedience to those required behaviors must be punished to reinforce the standards and to instruct those who disobey.

Applying the characteristics of middle school students to their education does not mean that the school is erratic, moody, or searching for a self-identity as many, most, or all of the students are on any school day. It is productive to apply the energy, the curiosity, the variety, the attitude of discovery, and the dynamism of the students into the educational experiences that are designed exclusively for the middle school students and more precisely for the unique group of middle school students who are being taught today in the 6th grade math class, in the 7th grade science class, or in the 8th grade social studies class.

Then what happens? Fewer battles and more learning. Given the reality of the characteristics of middle school students who are moving through the ups and downs, the zigs and zags of the middle school maze, middle school teachers who apply the energy, curiosity, and wonder of the middle school students can accomplish much more with their students, for their students, and in their teaching career than can an educator who struggles to impose silence, stillness, worksheets, and a daily routine of the unimaginative.

This is not to say that the middle school becomes a perpetual playground or that the classroom becomes an amusement park. The adults at school are in charge. The curriculum must be mastered. Real work must be done. Drill and practice will be needed. Traditional teaching methods can work as part of the overall variety of instructional activities. A teacher who creates teaching techniques that productively apply a 7th grader's energy and curiosity will see more results than a teacher who resents and repels that energy and curiosity.

Consider two 8th grade social studies teachers whose students are studying the Constitution of the United States. One teacher has spent time to make copies of the Constitution for each student with the most important parts underlined. This teacher has five worksheets with questions on the front and back of each sheet. One worksheet will be done each day Monday through Friday. The next Monday a long, detailed video about the Constitution will be shown. The test on the Constitution will be on Tuesday.

The activities are designed, the teacher says, "To cover all of the material. We have to move at a steady pace. And, well, my classes this year tend to get disorderly unless I pour on the paperwork for them to do. I have to keep them busy and I have to keep them quiet. It's the only way to manage groups like these and some of them still get in trouble for talking or bothering someone else or not following instructions."

Another middle school social studies teacher has different plans for her students. She challenged her 8th graders to write a Constitution for their school. The document had to include details about the school's legislative, executive, and judicial branches. The students had to interview administrators, teachers, staff, students, parents/guardians, and community members. The students had to get information about school district policies and school rules.

After the constitution for the school was written, the students created a ten-minute video for the entire school to watch. The video included a short debate between a student who was very much for the constitution and a student who presented reasons to oppose the constitution. Two days later, each first period class in the school had a vote on the constitution. The entire document had been posted on the school's Web site and each teacher had a copy to share with students.

After the votes of all students, faculty, administrators, and staff had been counted, the results showed that 6th graders opposed the constitution, while 7th graders, 8th graders, and the collective group of administrators, faculty, and staff approved the constitution. The agreement had been that three of the four groups had to ratify the constitution for it to be implemented.

The 8th grade social studies class now worked for several days in the library, in the computer lab, and in the classroom to compare and contrast their process of writing and ratifying a constitution with the process that was actually used in 1787 and 1788. The students also compared and contrasted the content of the two documents. The results were so good that students asked, "Back then they added a Bill of Rights. Can we do that, please? Can we write a school bill of rights?" What would your answer be to that question from those students?

Consider the experiences that teachers would have in the examples above. At the end of the week of worksheets, what sense of accomplishment will the teacher have from distributing worksheets, watching students as they do or do not complete the worksheets, and then grading the rote writing on the worksheets?

At the end of the constitution activity what experiences will that teacher have had as she continuously interacted with the students, answered their questions, guided their efforts, ensured that everyone participated, max-imized the unpredictable learning moments as they emerged, and evaluated the creative work of students to be sure that they learned the required curricu-lum content? For this teacher, the students asked if they could do more work to extend the learning adventure into a bill of rights. How likely is it that the other students asked, "Please could we have another week of nothing but being still, being quiet, and filling in blanks on more worksheets?"

The middle school students benefit when teachers apply the most useful of middle school characteristics into the lesson plans and lesson activities. Middle school teachers also benefit from using unique middle school teach-ing methods because productivity increases, behavior problems with students lessen, and the teacher has a more meaningful career experience. The students learn and behave better. The teacher causes more learning and manages the classroom more effectively. Everyone wins so why do anything else?

Consider these opposing perspectives. "I wish we could do some creative activities. I know the students would like some variety. I hear other teachers talk about the neat stuff they do. Well, I mean, if my students would ever sit down and be still and get quiet long enough to listen we might be able to do something creative."

"I used to think that if students would sit down and quit talking, then we could do something really neat. What I learned is if we do something really neat, that is what gets their attention, their interest, their cooperation, and their commitment. My classroom is not games or play. We work and we learn. The ways we work and the ways we learn fully occupy all of the student's energy and curiosity."

"There is rarely a behavior problem because they are so interested in our activities that they have no reason to misbehave. So, I don't wait for middle school students to sit down and be quiet permanently. I fascinate them with a variety of activities, including some very basic drill and practice, that gives them all they could ask for as 7th graders who tend to be vibrant, interactive, and energetic."

What about the middle school students who are shy, who are reclusive, who are loners, who are not curious or are not energetic? The alert middle school educator will be sensitive to this. Some middle school students are advanced in maturity and have moved beyond some of the challenges of the middle school maze. Some middle school students may be overwhelmed by the many differences in middle school versus elementary school and their only way to cope is to minimize interaction with people because the whole experience and atmosphere are just too much to adjust to. Other middle school students may be experiencing family difficulties, health problems, learning barriers, or growing-up problems that make it difficult to eagerly concentrate on school, on learning, on making friends, and on being involved.

Middle school students do have a collection of characteristics that are expected in 6th, 7th, and 8th graders; however, each student has his or her own degree of each characteristic. Also, each student has an individuality that has developed in part and is developing further through these a-maze-ing years. Middle school educators who are aware of and sensitive to the individuality of each student can develop responses that work for each student and that address each student.

Knowing the middle school students collectively is important. Knowing your middle school students individually is an advantage that middle school educators can give themselves to help maximize the achievements of the students and to more fully create meaningful career experiences for educators.

In a middle school where each class meets daily, teachers have the opportunity every day to learn more about each student. A skeptic might ask, "With everything I have to do, how can I be expected to know much about each student? I mean, with six classes of 7th grade English to teach, I have 158 students—158 lively, moody, immature twelve-year-olds and thirteen-year-olds. Keeping everything under control and covering all the curriculum—just doing that takes all my time and energy.

"How can I get to know much about 158 students when I have some who read at a 4th grade level and some who read at the 10th grade level sitting in the same class? Improving their reading or giving them new challenges in reading, that takes time. I need to know their reading skills, not their life story."

Does the teacher realize the idea within her last statement? She and the 7th grade social studies teacher could team up for a project called "Your History." Each student writes a paper that includes the following information uniquely written by each individual student:

1. Where and when you were born. The cities where you have lived through your life.
2. Describe a situation from childhood when something happened that taught you a very important lesson.
3. Think about your elementary school years. Describe your most important achievement from those years. It could be something you accomplished through school or through something else.
4. Talk with someone from another generation who knows you well. It could be a family member, a friend, or a neighbor. Have them tell you what they think your best achievement has been.
5. Think about the next ten years. What would you like to accomplish in school? What job, career, or profession are you most interested in?

The "Your History" assignment could include writing a rough draft and then going to the computer lab one class at a time to type the papers. The English teacher can work with students on the writing process as rough drafts become finished products.

The social studies teacher can read all of the papers when they are finished in typed form. An emphasis could be that historians use multiple sources to research history. When the students ask someone to provide insight about an important achievement, they do the type of multiple source research that historians do. Each student is an expert on his or her life, but hearing from another person about an achievement in that life will be revealing as historical research always is.

As the teachers read these papers, which are fully valid academically, the teachers are also getting to know more about each student. Teaching the students and getting to know the students need not be two different endeavors that compete for limited time.

If a middle school has seven hundred students and two guidance counselors, there are 350 students per counselor. How does one middle school counselor get to know 350 students? Perhaps the 6th graders could do a version of the "Your History" project that they will save on the computer at school and update when they are in 7th grade and again in 8th grade. This project becomes a writing process that spans three years and that helps evaluate writing progress.

The counselors could read the papers that the 6th graders write as a way of getting to know the new students. They could also read the papers of 7th and of 8th graders to get reacquainted with returning students and to meet the new 7th or 8th graders.

The counselors may visit classes to provide information and to provide instruction. The counselors could work with the health teacher to present a certain lesson together. The counselors can visit the cafeteria during lunch to interact with students. Of course, the counselors would spend time each day with students, individually or in very small groups, as circumstances, situations, problems, or problem prevention needs arose.

With continued efforts, some by intentional design to be with students and others as guidance intervention, the counselors can get to know the students despite a high, probably much too high, ratio of 350 students—or more in some places—to one counselor.

The common expectation is that because middle school principals and assistant principals manage discipline matters, they will get to know the students who are sent to the office due to misbehavior. The students who do behave also deserve to be known by the administrators, plus for their benefit and career satisfaction, the school administrators need to know the students who are behaving well, who are making good grades, who are contributing in wholesome ways to school life.

Principals and assistant principals in a middle school will be told about students who violate instructions, rules, and the code of conduct. Discipline referrals or an equivalent communication will be provided to administrators as infractions occur. What about the many students who obey the rules, who make good grades, who work hard to improve, and who eagerly participate in worthwhile activities? How do the school administrators get to know these students and not spend all of their student interaction time with 6th, 7th, and 8th graders who cause discipline problems?

Ask for good news. To every problem there is an equal and opposite solution. If the problem for a middle school principal or assistant principal is that only bad news is communicated as in the discipline referrals, then create balance to that by having teachers or staff members communicate good news about students to school administrators so the administrators can acknowledge, support, and get to know those students.

Example: A 6th grader notices a five dollar bill on the floor in his science classroom. He picks up the money, gives it to the teacher, and explains that it is not his. A short time later another 6th grader in much distress and in tears comes to this science classroom and tells the teacher that she lost some money. The student gives the teacher enough information to convince the teacher that the money belongs to her. The student is at peace now knowing she has her money for lunch and to attend the school football game later that day. The teacher informs the principal of the honest action that one student did to turn in the missing money. The principal sees that student at lunch and gives the student a school t-shirt from a collection of shirts that were donated to the school precisely for rewarding students who do what is right.

By seeking good news, the school administrators help affirm the many students who behave well, do their work, and cooperate daily. The middle school students share this characteristic with people of all ages—they appreciate being noticed for doing good work. Teachers who arrive at school early or who stay at school late appreciate a thoughtful word from the principal about their commitment. Staff members who go the extra mile appreciate being noticed.

As a middle school creates that atmosphere of caring enough to acknowledge good behavior, good work, and acts of kindness or acts of honor, the school builds upon the need of middle school students to be noticed, to be acknowledged, to be guided in learning "who I am" or "who I can be."

With very rare exceptions of students whose progress through school is several years behind the expected schedule, middle school students are not old enough to get a driving permit, a driver's license, or a part-time job. Some middle school students may babysit, mow lawns, or do similar types of work for which they are paid, but it would be rare to see a middle school student in the common middle school age group working formally for an employer.

This means that middle school students are not distracted by the possibilities that come with access to a car. This also means that middle school students are not allocating ten hours, twenty hours, or more per week at a job. Those work hours are time when studying is not done, when homework is not done, when energy is absorbed. Those work hours can fill a significant amount of the nonschool time during the typical week for some high school students.

Before the driver's license, the part-time job, and other nonschool uses of time that come with the high school years begin, the middle school student can give school the time and the priority that are needed to maximize learning.

Of course, some high school students excel in academics while also being involved in school activities, having a part-time job, and driving a car. Other high school students put so much time and effort into their car, their job, their sport, or their club that grades decline and rather than maximizing learning, their goal is to pass.

The middle school years are a time to navigate the maze that challenges all who enter, yet that can fascinate and develop all who persist through the maze's challenges to exit successfully. A middle school student's energy, curiosity, attention, and effort can be concentrated on curriculum mastery plus the personal growth experiences associated with school. This can be done without the competing priorities that will soon be part of that same student's experience during the high school years.

By age eleven, twelve, thirteen, or fourteen, the middle school student brings sufficient life experience and school experience to attain mastery of or to confirm mastery of the academic basics and then to advance much further than those basics. These a-maze-ing years can be highly productive, meaningful, and useful in ways and in amounts that apply opportunities that may never exist at any other age, be it younger or older.

What an elementary school student is too young or too inexperienced to do, to learn, or to master, the middle school student is now old enough and educated enough to do, to learn, and to master. What some high school students are too distracted by or too uncommitted to do, to learn, or to master, the middle school student is young enough and interested enough to concentrate on, work on, and learn.

For educators who will apply the characteristics of middle school students into the learning process and who will create experiences that compel commitment, the middle school years can be unsurpassed in productivity and in importance. The learning quality and quantity can be superior for students. The career experience and satisfaction can be vastly rewarding for educators.

Maximize the middle school moment. The middle school moment is that vital time in the academic experience of students when the certain dynamics of a vibrant time of human growth and development can meet the equally certain adventurous set of experiences at school that maximize the learning of academics, self, life, and character.

Good habits that have not been formed yet can be acquired by middle school students during these amazing years. Bad habits that have been formed already can be corrected in middle school students. By the high school years, good habits that are missing in a student can still be acquired, but that is more difficult because the fifteen-, sixteen-, seventeen-, eighteen-year-old high school student's habits are becoming more engrained or entrenched.

Yes, high school students can reverse prior errors, can turn their lives around to get back on the proper path; however, getting that done earlier in the middle school years is more efficient and more likely to work than attempting to do that after the middle school years merely added three more years of strengthening bad habits, bad attitudes, bad behaviors, and a generally oppositional approach to school.

What is to be done given the reality of a society that values athletics more than academics, that celebrates movie stars instead of star teachers, that has created political and economic problems that defy simple solutions, that ignores problems rather than confronts problems, and that increasingly wonders why reading scores by students are not improving in a world of superficial pop culture that gets much more media attention than reading, writing, and arithmetic get?

Do what you can where you are with what you have. Maximize the middle school moment. Maximize that three-year time period when a sufficient foundation of prior education and prior life experience combined with a surge of energy, curiosity, and openness, which the eleven-, twelve-, thirteen-, and fourteen-year-olds have in abundance, create moments each day for unlimited academic achievement, personal growth, and completion of essential steps through the middle school maze.

Ask Brian Robertson about middle school. Brian is a junior in high school. He makes great grades, he is in several clubs, he is the school newspaper editor, and he is on the school's academic team that competes in quick-recall events. Brian can give some important insights into the middle school moment and the middle school maze.

I was lost in 6th grade. I had done pretty well in elementary school, but nothing great. I learned what children need to learn, you know, how to read and how to add and how to write. But I never did as well as most of my friends. School just never really mattered that much. My parents never came to school. They never read any books at home so neither did I.

When I started middle school it was a real shock. There were five hundred or so students in my elementary school and as 5th graders we thought we dominated the place. Then I was in this middle school of seven hundred or eight hundred students and the 6th graders were all lost in the crowd. The 8th graders were so big and there were so many of them. I could never get my locker to open. I could not find my classes. I kept forgetting lunch money.

The 6th grade classes were really tough for me. I mean, these teachers kept giving us more and more work to do. I had just about never done any homework. Who cares about grades in elementary school? Now, I had tons of work to do for 6th grade, but I didn't do the work. I figured it was no big deal. I would get by. Then we got report cards in October of my 6th grade year. I had flunked just about everything. I did have an A in band because I was naturally talented with music. I play drums and it just comes easily to me.

My parents told me to get the grades up or they would come sit in classes with me. I had heard stuff like that from them before, but, well, a friend of mine in 6th grade actually had to go through a day when her mother went to all of her classes. And that was because she had some C grades. So, I didn't want my parents to hear about that mother and think that parents really did come to school. I got my grades up to D or C level. I never made an A or B grade that year except in band.

Everything changed in 7th grade. I mean everything. There was this new teacher in 7th grade math and I got put in his 7th grade math applications class. That means I was in the slow class. The other 7th graders were in algebra or pre-algebra. I was in the math-for-students-who-can't-do-math class.

Actually, I could do math fairly well, but what's the point of all those math problems and stuff? All teachers ever did was give us math worksheets to do. Math seemed pretty useless to me. My job interest then was to drive a truck for some big national company. I knew enough math to figure out the miles to the next city or the cost of fuel. That was all the math I needed.

Well, Mr. Nathan Adams thought that math was the most important thing in the world. He was young and always happy to be at school. He told us we would actually do algebra in the second half of the year, but first we needed to know the basics of math. He was honest. He said that a bunch of tests we took in 6th grade showed that our math skills were not good. We had to fix that. He would make sure it got fixed, he promised us on the first day of school. I guessed he meant we would have twice as many math worksheets as we had in 6th grade. I was wrong. I was so wrong.

Mr. Adams never gave us a worksheet, well, never unless he made it up for us. We did all kinds of math problems that had our names in them. I remember one problem about a truck driver named Brian. It had all sorts of calculations about costs per mile, changes in fuel prices, costs to rent a truck or to buy a truck, and even problems about managing a trucking business. Another day the problems were all about music because some of us in math class were in the band. I had never noticed any math in music before.

So, Mr. Adams got our attention. He made math worth learning. By the end of the first semester we were ready for pre-algebra. The first day of the second semester, it was a really cold day in January, we did all sorts of algebra calculations using college basketball statistics that Mr. Adams had worked on during Christmas vacation. Then we used algebra to analyze the basketball statistics for the teams at our school. We came up with math explanations for why our teams won certain games and why they lost other games. It was really neat.

By the end of 7th grade I had an A in math. I took some fancy test and it said I was ready to take geometry in 8th grade. Imagine me in geometry as an 8th grader. Well, that's what I did and my grades were good, almost always a B and sometimes an A. It really helped that Mr. Adams taught my 8th grade geometry class. My middle school likes to do that so sometimes we had the same teacher two years in a row for math or for English classes.

So in high school 9th grade was not the shock that 6th grade had been. I was in another new school like when I moved to middle school, but high school just seemed easier to get used to. Maybe it helped that I was in the marching band and we practiced in July and August before school started so I knew a lot of people.

I think what really helped was that Mr. Adams got in touch with the high school math teachers and told them exactly what we had done in 7th and 8th grades. He gave them copies of our work. My 9th grade math teacher did some things like Mr. Adams did and other things were different. Still, it all fit together and it all made sense.

Now, I'm a high school junior. I'm taking calculus. I still am interested in trucks, but my goal is to be an engineer who designs better vehicles that use less fuel or new fuels and that are really safe. I have started looking at engineering programs at colleges. I think that has all happened because there was this one moment in that first day in 7th grade when Mr. Adams changed my attitude about math. He kept working on that for two years with me and with everyone else. Now, I make great grades, I like math, and I'm going to college. It all started in 7th grade.

I wonder sometimes what would have happened if Mr. Adams had not been my math teacher in 7th and 8th grades. I do keep in touch with him whenever I get a report card so he knows how well I am doing in school. I think he made all this happen. He tells me I did the work. Yeah, I have worked hard, but Mr. Adams convinced me that the work was worth it. School changed completely from 7th grade on. Thanks, Mr. Adams.

Optimistic? Yes. Possible? Yes. Who accomplished more, Brian or Mr. Adams? Wrong question. They both accomplished a lot that was important, meaningful, and impactful. Brian has developed a different attitude about school, he thinks about math in a new way, he expects more of himself, he makes good grades, and he has a direction that links middle school with high school and beyond.

Mr. Adams did his work with more energy and with higher standards than his contract or his employer require. Ask Mr. Adams what he does and his answer will explain what he does and why he does it a certain way. "I don't see myself as a math teacher. I don't teach math. I teach people about math. It's the people, those 7th and 8th graders, who matter most of all. If you get the people part of teaching middle school right, the math part will follow."

For Rachel Carlton 7th grade math was an entirely different experience.

Well, you know, it was just another class. There was nothing awful about it. I've had classes like that before. We had a new teacher. Well, like, she was not really a new teacher, but she was new at our school. Somebody told me she had taught for a long time at a high school. Something happened and she got moved to our school. She kept telling us how immature and lazy we were. I guess she thought, you know, we would be embarrassed by that name-calling. It never worked.

So, the class started bad and never really changed. All we ever did was problems from the book. She would assign twenty or thirty problems for us to do in class. Then she worked on the computer or graded papers or walked around. When we had questions she usually told us to try harder. If you don't understand it, when you try harder you just make mistakes faster. So, nobody learned much math.

Then there was this one week when the teacher was absent. We had a great substitute. She was retired from teaching. She told us that she taught middle school math for thirty-three years. Well, she was so cool. I loved that week.

During that week we did grocery store math and mall math and television math. She had all of these ads from stores and from a mall. We used Web sites that stores had. We used catalogs and online stuff. We did more math work that week than the rest of the year, I mean we learned more math that week. We even did restaurant math to use algebra to figure out what prices to charge for stuff on the menu.

Then our regular teacher came back. The substitute must have told her how good we were and how hard we worked because she said something like, "I hope that means you are more mature and less lazy now."

I don't want to sound mean, but I think our teacher was not very mature and, well, you know, like she was pretty lazy. All she did was tell us the page number and the problems to do. Maybe she did one sample problem on the board, but then she graded papers or did something at the computer.

So when I went to 8th grade math I was really worried. During all of 7th grade I had learned only one week of math. The 8th grade teacher must have heard about our 7th grade teacher. She never said anything about that, but I just figured it out. She told us that the first month of 8th grade math was to refresh our memory about 7th grade math. The truth is, I had just about nothing in my memory from 7th grade math. I think the teacher knew that.

So, 8th grade math was so cool. We used the computer. We played math games. We used the school building and measured everything there was. Then we did all kinds of neat stuff with those measurements to design a renovation for the school. We worked with the cafeteria ladies to see how they use math. We met with the school bookkeeper to learn about money math. We analyzed sports statistics.

There was an election for president that year and we did so much work on voting results. I learned tons of math. Our 8th grade teacher never told us that we were immature or lazy. I wondered about that. Why did one teacher think we were immature and lazy when, you know, another teacher thought we were like really smart and that we could learn anything. I don't know that answer, but I know the answer to any 8th grade math question.

Now I'll be in high school next year. The high school counselors met with us to talk about what classes to take. I want all the math I can get. I want that fancy type of math, algebra and geometry. I don't know what calculus is, but if they teach it, I'll take it. My 8th grade math teacher told me she thinks I could make a career out of math. My 7th grade math teacher never said that. Well, it worked out.

I'm just glad my 7th grade math teacher retired. I have a sister in the 6th grade and I sure didn't want her to have my 7th grade teacher. Somebody said that she just needed one year before she could retire and my 7th grade year was that one year. I guess that happens. I don't know anything about that stuff. I know I'm not immature or lazy. How could I do so much in 8th grade if I was immature or lazy?

Would it make sense to say, "Middle school—love it or leave it"? Perhaps it makes more sense to say "Middle school—love it or do not select it as a place to work to begin with." The second option avoids a difficult, frustrating, counterproductive mismatch.

Collectively, middle school students are quite different from elementary school students and are quite different from high school students. Lamenting those differences will change nothing. Wishing that the middle school students were as orderly as elementary students waiting perfectly quietly in a line will not change the likelihood of some eleven- to fourteen-year-olds to move in and out of a line, to touch someone in the line, or to walk backward instead of forward as the line advances.

Maybe, middle school line walking could have some creativity in it while also requiring cooperation. Perhaps walking backward offers insights about perspective that could apply in art class or science class. Putting middle school characteristics, idiosyncrasies, energy, and curiosity to good use is practical and is beneficial. Why fight a battle over proper conditions for a line when the line movement from classroom to cafeteria could, if a line is used at all, be instructional and productive as long as it is safe and managed?

Wishing that the middle school students were as progressed as high school students will not change the reality that in academics, in self-identity, in personal discipline, and in human growth and development, the middle school students are generally years behind the high school students. Time cannot be accelerated. Maturity in many parts of life moves at an incremental pace that rarely can speed up.

High school teachers might say that their students still have much to learn and still have many skills to acquire, yet the high school students overall are not merely older than middle school students, rather, they have moved through the a-maze-ing years and through the middle school maze into a new set of opportunities, a new set of challenges, and a different time of growth.

There are many wonderful, meaningful, rewarding, and unique possibilities of middle school. Middle school students, teachers, counselors, administrators, and staff can work together in a managed atmosphere and in a designed experience that applies, builds on, and utilizes the unique characteristics of middle school students. This does not mean that a vibrant twelve-year-old is allowed to run around the school, but the author worked with a twelve-year-old who was allowed to run in the gym daily during lunch for three minutes. Once that plan started, the student did not get in trouble again for disrupting classes due to his excess energy and movement.

The adults are in charge, yet the wise adults will be realistic and optimistic. These adults will thoroughly know their middle school students as a group and as individuals. These wise middle school educators will create and, as needed, re-create the educational atmosphere and the educational experience that works best with and for middle school students. Knowing the unique characteristics of middle school students and accepting the reality of those characteristics can be a magnificent foundation for a middle school, providing the education that students need and the career experience that educators seek. In the next chapter we explore further how to make that happen.

Chapter Two

The Essential and Unique Work of a Middle School

Middle school work builds on elementary school work, but middle school is not elementary school extended. Similarly, elementary school is not merely preparation for middle school. Elementary school has its unique opportunities, objectives, and responsibilities, given the needs of and developmental characteristics of children.

If a school had the grades of kindergarten through 8th grade, it is reasonable to expect that there would be some different rules for, experiences for, standards for, duties of, classes for, and opportunities for the students in grades 6, 7, and 8 as contrasted with kindergarten through 5th grade. Such distinctions help confirm the essential and unique work of a middle school.

Because of the unique middle school characteristics, what must a middle school do and be? The following insights come from the middle school educators who were surveyed for this book when they were asked a follow-up to the initial question, "What is the most unique characteristic of middle school students?" The follow-up question was "Because of that unique middle school characteristic, a middle school (a) must and (b) must not _____."

The survey respondents stated that a middle school must do and be the following:

- "Provide a wide array of educational and social experiences with emphasis on interpersonal connections."
- "Be flexible to meet a wide range of needs; must have a strong support staff including counselors and social workers."
- "Middle school students must be given time to exercise, even if it is walking around the parking lot with a class."

- "Foster an environment that promotes structure while allowing students opportunities to develop and explore their interests. This should include support for those who do not seem to be self-motivated."
- "Be prepared for 'neediness' of the students and for the parents of 6th graders."
- "Engage students in very motivating activities to help them go through this important part of their life."
- "Be developmentally responsive with strong guidance and support services."
- "Pay attention to how students feel they are perceived by others."
- "Build relationships with students and parents."
- "Build relationships with students, families, and the community, making education and hard work important priorities."
- "Be flexible, open-minded, caring, and safe."
- "Treat students as individuals."
- "Get to know every student and be ready for anything."

The survey respondents stated that a middle school must not do and must not be the following:

- "Not be treated as a 'miniature' high school."
- "Not be rigid, cold, unapproachable."
- "Students must not be forced to sit through lecture after lecture all day long. Stand-up breaks within the classroom are advisable."
- "Must not ignore student concerns regarding their peers and teachers."
- "Not assume students will get things on their own. Guidance is necessary at all levels. Keep checking on them."
- "Must not be cold and uncaring."
- "Must not stereotype what the personality of a successful middle school student should be. A quiet student could be depressed just the same as a student acting out."
- "Must not assume a 'one size fits all' approach to discipline and instruction."
- "Must not be condescending or assuming."
- "Must not be quick to judge students or unwilling to listen."
- "Must not assume that all students are to be dealt with in the same way."
- "Must not judge a child based on one day."

Relationships. Individuality. Concern. Variety of instructional methods. Flexibility. Physical movement. Structure. Connections with families. Support. Guidance. Knowing the students. These descriptions, priorities, and factors can help guide how the essential and unique work of a middle school should be done.

Because the work that must be done during the middle school years is essential and is unique, the middle school cannot be merely advanced elementary school or a preview of high school. Essential work and unique work require essential actions and unique approaches. How is this done?

The survey tells us that middle school must have these areas of emphasis: relationships based on concern and built individually; structure with support systems and flexibility as needed and variety as helpful; knowledge of students and connections with their families. These approaches make the middle school maze a journey that can be completed with success, meaning more ups than downs, more forward movement than backward, more academic achievement, and more personal growth.

Add to those areas of emphasis a sense of urgency that is based on these concepts:

(1) The older a student gets the less likely he or she is to finally develop good study habits, a good school work ethic, and obedience to school rules. Students who master the proper habits, form a strong work ethic, and expect themselves to be obedient in elementary school will accomplish more in elementary school and beyond than students who do not master those standards.

For students who have not mastered those standards when they enter middle school, it is vital that the proper habits, work ethic, and behavior become ingrained during the middle school years. Why? Because entering high school without having mastered those standards can quickly put a student at risk of not graduating from high school or of barely graduating with minimal passing grades, but little real education.

The middle school setting—fewer students, use of teaching teams, more structure, more support—creates a time and place such that struggling, failing, or low-achieving students can catch up with more likelihood than would occur in high school. A student who barely passed elementary school and who barely passes middle school is in a position to barely pass or not pass high school classes.

(2) Students who have established good academic habits, an honorable work ethic, and proper behavior can be given advanced, creative, accelerated, enriched experiences in middle school that expand their current and future possibilities.

(3) Students who have always done ordinary work—never failed, but never excelled—could improve during middle school years or could just maintain the same ordinary results. If the middle school years are three more years of ordinary grades with ordinary work ethic, average academic habits and fair behavior, it seems likely that high school would also be filled with four more years of ordinary results.

Middle school is not the last chance for failing students to improve, for successful students to excel, or for average students to reach higher levels, but middle school could be the last good chance for those desired results. If not the last good chance, middle school has a better chance of causing those desired results than does high school.

What is not corrected or maximized in middle school becomes harder to correct or maximize later. The middle school moment is unique and vital. The middle school years are unique and vital. The middle school experience must, therefore, be unique because it is essential and it is vital.

To further explore, understand, and know the essential and unique work of a middle school, some 6th, 7th, and 8th graders will introduce themselves in these pages. Please notice their perceptions of school, their ideas, their awareness, and their reasoning. Certainly they have more to learn about school and at school, yet their experiences and their attitudes are revealing.

My name is Melinda. I'm in the 6th grade. I should be in the 7th grade, but my parents made me repeat 5th grade. I really hated that because my friends went to middle school and I had to stay in the stupid elementary school for an extra year. The problem was reading. I never could read very well. My parents read a lot. My older brother is in 9th grade but he reads as much as my parents. My younger sister is in 4th grade and she reads better than me, but I'm getting there.

So I had to repeat 5th grade, which was really embarrassing. I mean, I had already done everything, I just did it really bad. The second time in 5th grade was so dull. I spent lots of extra time with a reading teacher. I finally did well on some reading test and everyone was happy about that. Now, I'm in 6th grade and I have this really neat idea. I want to be in 8th grade next year. I already asked my parents and they don't much like the idea. My school counselor says it is not likely or something, you know, really unusual would have to happen.

Well, I told them I would make straight A's in 6th grade. Then they would know I could skip 7th grade. My friend had a neat idea. She said I should be a 6th grader for half of this year and a 7th grader for the other half of the year. Why can't my parents and my school counselor think like that?

You might be interested to know that I really am making good grades. My mother says I needed that extra year in elementary school to mature and to prepare for middle school. I don't know about that stuff, but I know I want to catch up with my friends.

I have noticed something about 6th grade. It is so easy. Most of what we do is dumb stuff from books or worksheets except for science. My science teacher is cool. She says we are going to be real scientists every day in class. We almost never use the book. We do stuff, you know, experiments or lab stuff. I even checked out a book from the library about some famous lady scientist. Maybe that's what I'll become. If all of my classes could be like my science class I would do great in school. Why don't the other teachers do things like we do in science?

Oh, yeah. I almost forgot. I decided to stay out of trouble this year. I mean I'm older than everyone in my class. They seem so little and kind of lost. I don't much like these little 6th graders even though I'm a 6th grader. I think of myself as an almost–7th grader. Just give me some test and I can show that I know the 6th grade stuff.

Except for science, in my other classes we never do anything new or hard. For one week when school started we practiced unlocking and opening our lockers. Who needs to practice that for one week? I heard one teacher say it made her day go faster if all her classes had to practice with lockers. I don't get that.

So that's all I know to tell you. I don't much like school or dislike school. It would help if I could be with my friends in 7th grade and it would be neat if my classes could be like science, where we actually do something and learn something new. I think 6th grade is too much like 5th grade and I had enough of 5th grade.

* * *

My name is Juan Carlos, but I go by Carlos. I'm in 6th grade. To be honest, I've been doing really well in school this year. It's all because of this school camp I came to last summer before school really started. My middle school has a one-week Adventure Camp for any new 6th grader. Some company pays for it so teachers are here and they have lunch with us.

The Adventure Camp shows us what middle school is like. We go to classes. We learn our way around the school. We meet people. We have homework to do. We even talk to 7th graders and 8th graders who are really good students. They tell us what we should do. They even tell us how to stay out of trouble.

So when 6th grade started I was ready. I could open my locker. I could find my classes. I saw people I knew. I knew where to catch my bus. I had already read a book from the school library that I got during camp. It's really been easy.

Now, there is one other thing. These 6th grade teachers are friendly, but they are serious. I mean really serious. Here's how I know. They never waste time. Like, I mean, in 5th grade I had a teacher who would give us free time most days. I asked a 6th grade teacher if we ever had free time and she said something like, "We always have more work to do. Free time is for week-ends."

All of the teachers here are like that. If we have four or five minutes left in class and it looks like we finished everything, they bring out some four-minute reading activity or a four-minute math problem, even if it is not math class. We might read or do math in any class on any day. We never waste a minute.

I'm not great in math, but, well, I'm not as bad as I used to be. Maybe it's those four-minute math problems that keep coming up in other classes every day. I never liked math, but it's not so bad now. My English teacher has these math word problems. We have to read so it is English but we do math. I really liked the one we read about the baseball player whose batting average went up after he started extra batting practice. The teacher told us that extra reading practice and extra math practice would work the same way.

So, 6th grade is pretty good. We work all the time, but there is this one thing next week that sounds neat. Instead of our regular classes, the teachers are planning a math something, what did they call it? Oh, yeah, a math decathlon. Our classes all day will do stuff with math, no matter what class. We'll have ten different math events during the day. I think my favorite will be basketball math in gym class, but food math at lunch could be pretty cool.

So, that's all I know. School is not bad. Actually it is going better than I thought it would. I had heard awful stuff about 6th grade. It's not really true. The teachers here aren't like what people told me. They make us work, but, you know, they make it interesting.

* * *

My name is Shelton. I'm in 7th grade. I'll be honest. The only thing at school I like is basketball. I made the team last year and I made the team this year. My friends tell me I'm the best player on the team. My teachers tell me that I need to work on my classes as hard as I work in basketball. Well, you know, their classes just, I mean, it's like, classes are dull and basketball is exciting.

I have this one teacher who shows a video almost every day. If it's not a video it's questions from the textbook. My basketball coach never shows us a video except of our games. No coach I've had gave us a book to read about basketball. We practice, we run, we do drills, we scrimmage. It's like in basketball you get better by actually playing basketball. Can't we do that in classes?

Now my English teacher is different from every other teacher. He says we have to learn to write all kinds of stuff like papers and essays. So, he told us to create a magazine. What is he thinking? I can't create any magazine. Then he brought some magazines to school and showed us one about the Civil War, one about money, one about fashion stuff, and one about sports. Well, now he's talking about something I know. He let me write a magazine about basketball.

I interviewed my coach. I got statistics about our team. I talked to teachers about when they played basketball on a team. I even talked to the teacher who always shows us a video. He used to play basketball for a college. I never knew that. He teaches history. He asked me if I knew the history of basketball. I never thought that history had anything to do with basketball, but it does. So I wrote a long article for my magazine about the history of basketball. I even got to talk to my history teacher's old basketball coach. He's retired, but he sure knows a lot about basketball. I made a great magazine.

Then something really weird happened. My history teacher told us to create a magazine about history. I thought he was kidding, but he was telling the truth. He took us to the library and to the computer lab. I like to watch basketball on television so I made my magazine about the history of television. It was so cool. I can't believe that people just had three channels back then.

For a week we worked on our magazines with no video and no questions from the book to get bored with. It was pretty neat. And you know what? That teacher started doing other new things. It was like the magazine woke him up. That's not all. We did a magazine in math. Then in science we did a video magazine. These teachers just went crazy with magazine projects. Nobody got tired of them because each one was different. We still had to read the textbooks and take tests and stuff, but those magazines were the best.

Somehow my basketball coach got all kinds of sports magazines from a university. He gave those to my English teacher and we got to read those after we finished other work. I was never much for reading until then. The librarian came to my English class and brought this cart full of books about sports and music and fashion and stuff we did our magazines on. I never knew there were all those books about basketball.

I actually learned a lot about basketball by reading. I thought I knew a lot, but the books knew more. We still run and drill at practice, but I think that reading made me work harder in the drills. So, you know, 7th grade is really good because of this neat stuff we get to do. I hope 8th grade will be like this.

* * *

My full name is Mary Margaret Eileen McGrady. My grandmother likes to call me Eileen because that was her mother's name. Most people call me Mary. Some people at school call me other names, mean names, but they get in trouble for that. Those mean people call everyone bad names. Why do they keep doing that? Can't somebody make them stop?

So, I'm in the 7th grade. Why are all of the 7th grade teachers so serious? It's like they are always mad. My cell phone rang once in math class and the teacher acted like I should be arrested. I think the students who call everyone mean names are a bigger problem than stuff like a cell phone ringing.

These teachers are so serious. I asked my science teacher once if he ever goofs off and he was shocked at my question. So he never goofs off, but I do. What's wrong with that? All of our teachers keep telling us about some new test we have to take at the end of the school year. It sounds like if we do really bad on the test we have to stay in 7th grade again. I can't imagine two years with these super-serious teachers, but maybe they are just trying to scare us.

I never had to repeat a grade so I doubt I'll fail that test. My grades are low; well, they are really low. All I need to do is pass. My mother owns a hair styling salon. I help out there on the weekends. When I finish high school I'll get trained to work full-time at my mother's place. School has nothing to do with that so if I could make the rules I'd really like to have nothing to do with school.

We did have one activity last year that I liked. I think it was called Career Day. There were like forty or fifty people who came to our school. They told us about their jobs. I went to the class that a police officer taught and then I heard a guy who owns a restaurant and then I heard some woman who has her own hair styling place. My mother has a better place. I could tell from the pictures this other lady showed. But it was interesting to hear her talk about how hard the work is. My mother never says that. Mom likes the work a lot and she says if you like your job it really isn't work.

I think my teachers don't like their job. They seem to work all the time, except when they are absent. Some of my teachers are gone a lot, like once a week or something like that. Do they still get paid when they are not here? Are they skipping school or is it something else?

We had this substitute teacher in math class last week. He was different from any teacher I ever had. He actually gave each of us a penny. Then he had all of these math problems about our money. He had something for us to read about the history of coins and how coins are made. Then we flipped the penny ten times to see if it was heads or tails. We put our heads and tails numbers on the board and did some neat stuff with all those numbers.

Then we talked about saving money. He told us to save one penny today and two pennies the next day and three pennies the next day and keep going. I thought it was pretty silly and no big deal, but he showed us a chart of how much money you save after one year. It was so cool. I should save like that someday.

Then the regular teacher came back the next day and she was so mad. The substitute was supposed to give us five worksheets, but something went wrong and nobody copied the worksheets so the substitute did that money stuff. My guess is the substitute knows that sometimes there is not much left by the regular teacher. I did wonder about all of that. How did the worksheets get lost or something? Somebody said the substitute got here really early and figured out what to do. I don't think many people get here early. I don't. I get here at the last minute. Why spend more time at school than you have to?

So is there anything at school that I like? I liked that substitute teacher in math. He should teach us all the time. I like lunch, well, the food is not too bad, but at least I get to talk with my friends. When we talk in our classes the teachers go crazy and tell us to get back to work. What's wrong with talking to friends?

I think we need recess so we can, you know, take it easy and talk. It would help me get through the day if we had recess. Why can't we do that? We have to sit in these rooms all day and be quiet and read stuff. What's wrong with a little recess? We had recess in elementary school and there was nothing wrong with that.

Well, that's all I know about school. I just want to finish middle school and high school fast. Then I can work with my mother at her shop. I wish I could get out of school faster. School just doesn't do much for me. I sure don't do much at school. Why not let somebody like me finish all of this stuff fast? I would work harder if I could finish faster. I'm not the only one like that, but nothing is going to change. I'm stuck here.

* * *

I'm Kevin. I'm in 8th grade. The people at my school say it's the best middle school in the state. We take these dumb tests every year and I guess, you know, like we do good on the tests or something. I don't know if we are the best in the state. I do know that there is one thing I really like about this school. Maybe two things.

I like taking high school classes and I mean for credit. The new principal got the idea that 8th graders were ready, well, some 8th graders were ready and others never do much anyway, but some 8th graders could do high school work. So our school has one group of about one hundred 8th graders who are in the Plus Program. It's like we are 9th graders. We can get four high school credits. Math, science, social studies, and English are the classes we take for credit. The other one hundred or so 8th graders just do regular 8th grade stuff.

Most of my friends are in the other 8th grade classes. They say it's a lot like 7th grade. Well, my classes are nothing like 7th grade. I have homework every night in every class. And most of the Plus students are smarter than me. So how did I get into the Plus Program? It wasn't my idea.

I was put in the Plus Program because my school counselor told my mother that teachers thought I was smarter than my grades were. I made C grades in almost everything. What's wrong with that? School never interested me much so I just did enough to keep going.

Now this counselor decides to change everything for me. I met with the counselor after we talked to my mother. I said that the nerd program was stupid. It would be all the smart 8th graders who are in the orchestra or who are in the chess club or who never get in trouble. You know, the students that teachers like best and give good grades to. I was not really interested.

Then he said something really weird. He said I might be able to finish high school in three years. That was the first time anybody ever said anything to me about getting out of school faster. That interests me. School is just not what I like. School is the same old stuff all the time.

Well, the Plus Program is not the same old stuff. It's more work, but it's different work. We have textbooks and worksheets and a video sometimes. But we do stuff. We have this activity every week when all one hundred Plus students are in the gym or in the library or maybe the cafeteria and we do, like, this big project.

My favorite was the giant map we made. It covered an entire wall in the cafeteria. We spent days getting stuff ready for it. We worked on it in all of our classes. I never thought there was much math or science in a map, but there is. And there is social studies and English in a map. So, we made this huge map of the earth and it's all over a wall in the cafeteria. Some newspaper guy came to take pictures and our map was in the newspaper. This is neat.

A college professor saw the picture and called the school. He came to talk to us about geography and science and maps and pictures of earth from space. I asked him how people get to go to a university. He said they take the hardest classes in high school and study a lot. I started wondering if I could do that.

I just wanted to get out of school until I heard that college guy talk. I still don't much like school, but maybe college would be better. I'm going to think about it some more, you know, and see what stuff people do in college. If I can finish high school in three years maybe I can finish college in three years and get out of school forever. I like that.

* * *

I'm Lucy. I go to Kevin's school. I'm in the regular 8th grade group. We have this joke where we call ourselves the Minus People. Our teachers really don't like it when we call ourselves the Minus People and stuff like that, but, like, I mean, it's true. The other group is Plus so we must be Minus. Actually, I'm as smart as any Plus student. I just don't do much work and nobody expects much from me. I just get by and don't cause trouble. I really don't care that much. We think Minus People is a pretty funny name.

My parents asked me what it meant. It doesn't mean anything. It's, like, it's just a name. We don't tease the Plus People, well, sometimes, but that stuff goes on all the time for one reason or another. We do talk about each other a lot, but it's not usually mean. We just hear stuff about people and we get curious. With cell phones and texting and stuff, rumors or gossip spread fast. It's no big deal.

Well, it was a big deal once. Some guy at school started a rumor that another guy was cheating on his girlfriend. It was all made up. The guy spreading the rumor was jealous. He liked the same girl that the other guy liked, but the girl did not like either one of them that much. She just wanted a boyfriend so she could be cool. It got really crazy. People made threats about a fight that was going to be in the cafeteria at lunch or maybe at a bus stop one morning.

The principal heard about it and everything got really serious. The principal got everyone involved together and made them sign a discipline contract. He made them work on stuff together, like sweep the halls and clean the cafeteria tables. He told their parents that there would be a three-day suspension from school or a parent of each of the biggest rumor spreaders could come to school and go to classes with their child for a day. All the parents came to school. The rumors stopped.

You can't imagine what this school was like on the day all of those parents came to class. Everybody behaved. I mean, like, everybody. The teachers loved it. To be honest, it was better to have those rumors stop. It was mean and it hurt feelings. A fight sounded exciting but, you know, sometimes fights at school get really ugly. So everybody learned about rumors.

Now, about the Minus People. I told my brother about the nickname we gave ourselves. He is really creative so he made up this neat idea. The Minus People are in regular math classes. The Plus People are in algebra and geometry. So my brother gets this idea. He said Minus stood for "Math Is Not Understood by Students." He's right. Math is stupid, especially fractions. Who cares about fractions?

So, I think the Minus People should be listened to. We are not dumb. We just think math is dumb and lots of other school stuff is dumb. No wonder people start rumors. It gives them something interesting to do. Which do you think an 8th grader would be more interested in? Rumors or math?

Now, there is one other thing I should tell you about middle school. I can't see much difference in 6th grade, 7th grade, and 8th grade. It's all the same kinds of stuff. I think all we do is 6th grade stuff over and over. Can't they come up with something different?

Middle school cannot be based on the results of a public opinion poll that measures what 6th, 7th, and 8th graders say they like and dislike about school. The adults know what needs to be done at school. The adults know the laws, the policies, the regulations, and the requirements of school and about school. The adults are in charge. What benefits could those adults get from listening to the likes and dislikes of students? Could that listening help those adults better realize and better implement what works best to address the essential and unique work of a middle school?

For example, the Minus People have made it clear that they do not like math. What does "Do not like math" mean? Part of what it means is "Math is confusing." Another part of what it means is "I'm no good in math. The smart students, the nerds, they do math." Another part is "Math at school is dumb. It's stupid problems to solve. When will I ever use that?"

Teachers of middle school students can answer the "when will I use that?" question with "now" if they connect middle school math with middle school life. Just look through the school. Where and how is math being used by students in their real life right now? Consider comments such as the following that could be heard from students in normal conversation at a middle school.

- "Can you believe that game? We hit all of our free throws. That's why we won."
- "I really want to see that new football movie, but it costs $8. Why do movies cost so much?"
- "I heard that the grading system might change. You can get a D with 65 percent now. It might change to 70 percent."
- "My dad wants to get a new car so my older brother can drive the car Dad has now. A new car costs a lot, but my brother has to pay for the insurance if he gets the old car. Insurance is something like $500 or more."
- "The band is selling candy. Want to buy some? We have to raise money for some new instruments."
- "This school pizza is not bad today. But I bet they would sell more if they got the pizza from a real restaurant. I think this stuff is just frozen and they heat it up."
- "My grade on that test was so bad. I never get low grades on science tests. 71! How did that happen?"
- "I saw the coolest shoes online yesterday. I've got to get them before the track season starts. It said they were 30 percent off this week."
- "Did you hear about that high school student the police stopped on the way to school? He was bringing his sister to our school, but, like, he was driving way too fast. He got a ticket and it was something like $150 and he has some driver school stuff to do."

- "Are you going on that field trip tomorrow? I think you should. That museum will be neat, plus we get to stop somewhere cool for lunch. I think it costs $5, but you have to pay today."
- "Could you believe it? The principal was so serious on the school news. He said that if for one week we average 98 percent attendance we get to have a dance at school and he said it would be free."
- "I heard somebody say that the library is getting ten new computers. They might sell the old ones. The old ones are still working. Maybe my parents could get one for me. It would be cheap."
- "He got suspended for two days. That's the third time he's been suspended this year. If it happens again he could get sent to another school."
- "No, I can't loan you a dollar. You still owe me from last week when you borrowed $2."
- "I heard that she made such a high grade on those tests we had to take that she might skip 8th grade."
- "I was two minutes late for school. So what? Why does that get me in trouble? They should be glad I came instead of just skipping the whole day."
- "Our bus is late again. I really have to get home. I have a piano lesson at 4:30 and it costs a lot of money. It ends at 5:00 even if I get there late."

The students who made those comments are using numbers to express thoughts. The students may not see these uses of numbers as being in any way similar to middle school math, but an astute middle school math teacher could make many connections between the math curriculum and the wholesome real life interests of students. Sports statistics, prices of products, school data, analysis of or interpretation of test scores, an individual student's grades as shown on a chart or graph, pizza prices, movie prices, and traffic tickets could be the topics of very interesting math problems to solve. The fact that they are real-world problems and interests can increase the importance of mastering math to students who like to ask the question: "When am I ever going to need to know this?"

Age-effective instruction encompasses more than age. The eleven- and twelve-year-olds in 6th grade share membership in the same age group; however, no two eleven- or twelve-year-olds are identical. These eleven- and twelve-year-olds are likely to share some characteristics, but they will vary in some ways or in many ways. Middle schools have essential and unique work to do.

Getting middle school right is vital. There is a better chance of breaking bad habits during the 6th, 7th, and 8th grade years than there would be in high school if those bad habits became further ingrained during middle school. There is a better chance of developing and expanding skills of successful students during the middle school years than there would be in high school if the successful student endured three years in middle school with no challenges, no adventures, and no new knowledge.

Knowing and responding to (A) the overall characteristics of middle school students and (B) the individual characteristics of each middle school student can help middle school educators achieve the desired results as they do their essential and unique work with middle school students. Two middle school students who are very different, yet amazingly alike, can provide some helpful insights into maximizing the essential and the unique work of a middle school.

So, my name is Alex. I'm supposed to tell you about middle school stuff. Well, I mean, like, 8th grade is OK. It's nothing great. You know, it's school. My teachers have no idea that I am going to compete next summer in a national agriculture contest. My family owns a small farm. That's where we live. I help raise sheep. It's hard work, but you can make money and I'd rather work with animals than most people I know. I have chores to do on the farm every day. I get it all done. I have to. The sheep count on me.

At school I get my work done, but other students do better than me. It's like, um, it's like they must study a lot. I know a lot of science from working on the farm, but the science work at school is not farm stuff. It's school stuff.

I'm also great with machines. My father taught me how to fix anything we use on the farm. It's really pretty easy. So why can't school include agriculture stuff and machine repair? There's something like that for high school students. But there's nothing like that for 8th graders. Why not?

Sometimes I do better work at school. Last year I was on the Iceberg team. That's a weird name. Usually the middle school teams are like Adventurers or Pilots or, you know, Seekers or something like that. So our team had five teachers and about 125 students. The teachers taught us math, science, English, social studies, and Spanish. The students were in groups of twenty-five and we rotated through the classes every day so we were with each teacher every day.

Well, at the start of 7th grade the teachers told us our team name was Iceberg. What was that all about? Then they showed us these really cool pictures of icebergs, you know, it was the type of picture that shows the little part above the water and the big part under the water. Usually you can't see the part under the water so maybe it was a drawing instead of a picture. Anyway, it was cool looking. We got t-shirts with the same picture painted on the front. The back of the t-shirt said "10% + 90% = Success."

What's that mean? I thought it was a stupid math problem, but it made sense after my science teacher explained it. They said that maybe 10 percent of an iceberg can be seen. The teachers were telling us that when they teach 7th graders they get to know only about 10 percent of the information about each student. They know our grades and our names and school stuff. They don't know that I am really smart about farm stuff. What they don't know is the 90 percent. They said they wanted to learn about that 90 percent.

They said 7th grade was going to be this big year to learn all kinds of math and science and other school stuff, but that's not all. They said our team would really get to know each other. They even said that each student could pick things to do that other students didn't do.

So I worked on projects about math for farms, science for farmers, social studies topics about farming, and in English class I read books about farming. In Spanish I learned vocabulary about farms. So, 7th grade was neat. The teachers got to know us really well and they kept their promise. Whatever they learned about us got included in our class activities a lot. Seventh grade was cool.

Eighth grade is not cool. The teachers had us vote on our team name. Somebody said we should be the Mountains because—this is so stupid— because we are climbing to high school. Somebody else said the perfect name would be Octagons since that shape has eight sides and we're in 8th grade. That was stupid too. So finally some new student said at her old school a neat team name was the Superstars. That caught on really fast and we picked that name.

Then for the first half of 8th grade we never did anything super and nobody felt like a star. Maybe we can change the name to the Dull and the Boring because that's what most of 8th grade has been so far. I'd be better off in 7th grade again or in 9th grade. Why can't my 8th grade teachers just do things the way my 7th grade teachers did? I mean, like, that stuff last year was neat and I learned a lot.

* * *

My name is Jennifer. I'm in the 8th grade. I love 8th grade. My school is so cool. I'm no genius. My sister is a genius. She is so smart. She is getting this huge college scholarship. I'm a good student. I was an average student in elementary school. In middle school a lot of stuff is different. I'm making good grades, all A's and B's. I never get in trouble. I hope high school will be like this.

My middle school goes crazy for people on their birthdays. If your birthday is during a vacation, they go crazy right before or right after the vacation. If your birthday is on a weekend, you get added to the Friday celebration. The cafeteria ladies bake cakes and on your birthday you get cake at your table in the cafeteria. It's so cool.

The teachers make every student write a story that tells about our life. They say it's like an autobiography. We write about the most important lesson we learned as little children and then in elementary school. We write about our best, you know, the best thing we've done, like winning some trophy or making money or getting our picture in the newspaper. Then we tell what we would like to do in high school and even after high school.

What's cool is that we read our paper every month. We add something we have done in 8th grade and we change our high school plans and stuff for after high school if we have new ideas.

I seem to work harder every time we rewrite that paper. Maybe it just makes me think more. Maybe it's because I learned something about high school. Usually it's because I have a new career goal. I used to want to be a lawyer, then a chef, then a singer, then a video game designer, then a politician, and now I think I like the idea of being a lawyer again. Whatever job we select we do a lot of reading about it. We write a report to show how math, science, English, social studies, and our other classes fit in with our career.

Then the teachers do something really cool. I don't know how they do this, but it is so neat. They create activities in our classes that help us learn about the career. What does math have to do with being a lawyer? Well, I found out that lawyers are businesspeople. Their business is law. I found out how they make their money. I also found out how much it costs to go to college and law school. I need to start saving money for that now.

So 8th grade is hard work. We have these awful spelling tests in every class once a week; science on Tuesday, math on Wednesday, English on Thursday, and social studies on Friday. The words come from our vocabulary list that grows each week in each class. Our teachers say that modern students can't spell because of texting and Internet stuff. Well, we work on spelling a lot. I can spell.

We even get up in class and do cheers or sing songs that help us spell. When a spelling word becomes a cheer or a song or a dance, you just remember it better. We film our cheers and stuff. Then we post it on our school Web site so our parents can see it. My mother always knows what spelling words to ask me about at supper every night. I guess lawyers need to know how to spell, so maybe it will help me. I know these spelling tests get old, but I am improving with spelling. These teachers make us learn. I guess that's how it has to be.

Which of these two 8th graders, Alex or Jennifer, is having an 8th grade experience that matches what the survey participants said a middle school must do and must be: relationships, individuality, concern, variety of instructional methods, flexibility, physical movement, structure, connections, support, guidance, knowing the students?

What is the impact on a middle school student who, year after year, has the type of experience that Jennifer is having as an 8th grader and that Alex had as a 7th grader? What is the impact on a middle school student who never has an educational experience like that of Jennifer in 8th grade and Alex in 7th grade?

How are the most valuable, impactful, meaningful, age-effective experiences for middle school students created and provided? The next chapter helps answer that question with the topic of middle school teaching and teachers.

Chapter Three

Middle School Teaching and Teachers

According to the survey responses listed below, we can identify what a new middle school teacher must know. The word "new" was included so experienced middle school educators could share their lessons from experience and reflection; however, these words of advice apply to the work done by new middle school teachers or by veteran middle school teachers. Survey participants were asked, "What must new middle school teachers know?"

- "Middle school students are unique and will test you in every way possible. Consistency and caring are two traits that all successful teachers have or develop."
- "National and state standards, instructional strategies to engage students, developing good teacher-student relationships."
- "A new middle school teacher must know that whatever programs or initiatives are in place at the time of your hiring, they will change or be eliminated to coincide with the latest novel idea to solve the riddle of the middle school student. They must also know that lesson planning time being provided during the school day is a myth."
- "If students smell fear, they will go for blood. It's better that you address any insecurities you may have about yourself before you enter a classroom. Students will be able to pick them out and use them against you. Unfortunately, we as adults try to make our personal issues into 'students being defiant' issues."
- "Get to know your students, especially their names, quickly. Do activities that help you get to know them. Have the students tell or write about themselves and ask parents or guardians to write about their child."

- "Research best practices related to the age group. De-escalation strategies. The content to be taught. Classroom management. Communication skills. Awareness of legal issues and procedures."
- "Pressures are very hard on teachers—504 plans, admission and release committees for special education, providing services for gifted and talented students, helping average students, dealing with lack of support from many homes. Plus, we have come to be a test-score driven system."
- "Every student is different and learns in different ways. Every student is a person."
- "Reliability, consistency, humor, and professionalism will serve your students and yourself well."
- "Be flexible and understanding. Build positive relationships with the students. Know the curriculum."
- "Establish a relationship. Establish support. Be yourself. Be consistent. Be tough, you can always let up later."
- "Try, try, and try again to reach out. Establish and follow routines."

The above insights emphasize knowing the students to be taught; knowing the subject matter to be taught; creating a structured system of instruction, of classroom rules, and of classroom procedures, yet being flexible as needed; and of simultaneously managing all of the organizational and operational duties that teachers are assigned. Doing all of that is not an eight-hour-per-day job, nor is doing all of that a five-day-workweek job. Despite some perceptions to the contrary, teaching well is not a nine-month-per-year job.

A place for current or prospective middle school teachers to begin is reality. When they arrive in your classroom on the first day of school, the middle school students with whom you will work this year are who they are and are what they are. Some of who and what they are is favorable, in some cases very favorable or exemplary. Some of who and what they are needs improvement, in some cases vast improvement or drastic improvement.

The realistic middle school teacher quickly identifies who and what her students are. This is followed by the implementation of a variety of instructional activities that begin the demanding, challenging, and vital journey through this year's portion of the middle school maze so the students make significant strides from who and what they are to who and what they can be.

Middle school is fertile ground for educational entrepreneurs. What does middle school teaching have to do with entrepreneurial activity? Entrepreneurs are energetic, creative, results-driven, determined people who refuse to accept today's conditions as the ultimate of what can be achieved. For students, the middle school years have some, if not yet all, of those entrepreneur attributes, especially energy and creativity.

The middle school teacher who is or who becomes an educational entrepreneur sees the classroom and the students as a dynamic work in progress that is directed by a carefully planned design, yet that can adapt realistically as new problems arise and opportunistically as new possibilities emerge.

Consider this approach. A middle school teacher decides to plan the entire school year prior to the first day of school. The teacher has a schedule that shows what pages in the textbook will be read and discussed throughout the year, day by day. The schedule shows when tests will be given on chapters in the textbook and on supplemental work. The schedule includes quizzes, projects, activities that conclude a unit, and visits to the library for research and extra reading. The plan for the year is precise, certain, and detailed.

Will this precision plan for the year work? Does this plan incorporate the unique characteristics of middle school students? Is this plan consistent with the ideas provided by the insights from survey participants who have been quoted in this chapter and prior chapters? Will the intended objectives of this teacher—to be efficient, to be productive, to be prepared—be reached through this prepackaged plan for the year?

This precision plan is unlikely to work. To be blunt, it will not work. The plan has some honorable intentions, and some planning prior to the start of the school year is mandatory. How effective can the planning be if the teacher is making plans for students whom the teacher has not yet met? "Oh, they are 7th graders. They'll be like last year's 7th graders. They'll be like 7th graders always are. The schedule from last year will be fine for this year." That will not work.

This year's 7th graders will share some characteristics with last year's 7th graders, but there will be important differences. The middle school teacher whose approach is that of an educational entrepreneur does not attempt to force, squeeze, push, and shove this year's 7th graders into a prepackaged prescription of instructional reruns from last year or last decade.

The educational entrepreneur is fascinated with the annual adventure that is new every year, of finding and creating the teaching methods and activities that work best with this year's students. The work of a teacher who teaches for thirty years is not to repeat year one over and over for twenty-nine more years. The work of a teacher is to realize that every year is year one. For this year's 7th graders, now is the one and only year to be a 7th grader. The educational entrepreneur thrives in middle school because the middle school students' characteristics invite and need the creative, bold, energetic, adaptive, organized, planned, structured, persistent approach of an entrepreneur.

The middle school teacher who is an educational entrepreneur plans thoroughly. Being creative does not mean arriving at school twenty minutes before classes begin on a Monday with an idea that came to your mind as you drove to school and that you intend to implement immediately. Consider that idea for a day or two. Put it on paper. Ask a colleague to review your idea.

Implement it on Wednesday after two days of thought and improvement. The creativity is still at work; in fact, it is more likely to be successful because it has developed and has been refined.

Planning is not the enemy of creativity. Planning does not prevent flexibility; rather, planning helps make it possible for a teacher to be flexible, yet to still know that schedules will be met and required work will be completed.

Know the students and know the subject were two areas emphasized in the survey responses. How does a middle school teacher get to know his or her students? Consider the following actions and then add more ideas to the list.

1. Assign the students an autobiography to write. Design this writing project so it invites authenticity. Require facts such as date and place of birth, but also require unique revelations such as "Describe a situation when you were very young when you did something that resulted in a very important lesson being learned."

2. Use the activity in which each student has to interview another student and then they switch roles. After that, the pairs of students introduce each other to the class.

3. Give the students an outline of a resume. It begins with name and address. It states an objective related to success in school this year. It includes prior achievements in elementary school. It includes interests, experiences, and achievements outside of school. It includes several references of people who know the student well. It could also include longer-term goals that relate to high school; education, training, or work after high school; career goals; and thoughts about future goals that are not related to career.

4. Instructional activities themselves are ways to get to know students. As a teacher calls on every student during a class period, some awareness of each student is begun and grows with further classroom interaction day to day.

5. Listen. As students enter your classroom, many of them will be talking to friends. Intentionally notice what they are saying, what interests them, what concerns them, what fascinates them, what confuses them, and what they are thinking about. The teacher may enter some of these conversations.

6. At school, go where the students go. Eat lunch in the cafeteria occasionally or, at least, spend some time during lunch in the cafeteria. Interact with students. During your planning period, perhaps visit another class of a teacher who is going to visit your class on another day. It can be very revealing to see your students in another classroom with another teacher. This is also a way to identify teaching methods you

can use. Attend athletic events, club meetings, concerts, and other school activities. Interactions with students at these events and with parents or guardians of students can be very beneficial.

7. Create an activity for the first and/or second day of school in which everyone in a class learns the name of each student in the class. This can be done as Ashley starts by giving her name. The next student says "Ashley, I am Stephanie." The next student says "Ashley, Stephanie, my name is Daniel." This continues until it returns to Ashley who then says the name of each student. The teacher does participate in this. A variation is to add one fact such as your favorite pizza topping. "I'm Ashley. I guess pepperoni." The next student says, "Ashley pepperoni. I'm Stephanie. Well, mushrooms." The pizza topping or other topic can help sometimes as a mnemonic device.

Getting to know the students is not limited to the opening days of the school year. This continues throughout the school year. The twelve-year-old 7th grader a teacher meets on the first day of school is not 100 percent identical to the thirteen-year-old almost–8th grader that same student has become toward the end of the school year. Getting to know the students means frequently updating that knowledge of each student. That comes as no surprise to and as no problem for an educational entrepreneur who intends for his or her teaching to always be the most effective it can be.

Given the acknowledged unique characteristics of middle school students, are there ways to get to know these students that are more effective than other methods? Consider the following two options and evaluate them for how effective they would be to help a middle school teacher get to know this year's students.

(1) Each student is given the following page to complete:

The questions below are provided so you can tell your teacher about yourself. For each question, select the answer that most accurately describes you. When you complete answering these questions, turn to pages 6 through 18 in our textbook and silently read those pages. Be sure to put your first and last name at the top of the page.

1. I am most like

   a. Summer
   b. Autumn
   c. Winter
   d. Spring

2. My favorite class at school is

a. Math
b. Science
c. English
d. Social Studies
e. An elective class (Tell which_____)

3. If I could be an animal I would be a

a. Dog
b. Cat
c. Lion
d. Fish
e. Bird

4. When I have free time I like to

a. play sports
b. read books
c. use a computer, video games, or cell phone
d. be with friends
e. work on my hobby

5. The best part about school is

a. classes
b. lunch
c. clubs
d. sports
e. seeing my friends

6. The worst part about school is

a. homework
b. tests
c. classes
d. rules
e. riding a bus

7. I expect most of my grades this year will be

a. A
b. B
c. C

      d. D
      e. F

8. Most of my grades last year were

      a. A
      b. B
      c. C
      d. D
      e. F

9. During summer vacation I like to

      a. sleep late
      b. work to earn money
      c. go to camp
      d. spend time with friends
      e. read

10. As far as homework is concerned, I

      a. always have it done on time.
      b. sometimes have it done on time.
      c. rarely have it done on time.
      d. never have it done on time.
      e. usually do it but forget to turn it in.

(2) The teacher checks attendance and then says to the students, "For about fifteen minutes today to begin class, we will get to know each other. It will take more than fifteen minutes on one day to really get to know each other, so we will continue this from day to day in various ways.

"For now, everyone stand up and be ready to move. You will talk to each other and find the person in the classroom whose birthday is the closest to yours. It might be the same day or it might be just a few days apart, but keep checking with people until you find the person with the birthday closest to your birthday."

The students talk, move, smile, listen, laugh, and get acquainted. Once the birthday pairs are arranged, the teacher says, "Now, in the pairs you have just created, think of what would be the perfect birthday party for each of you. It might be two separate parties, one for each of you, or you might prefer to get together and have one party for both of you. Take two minutes and create the parties or the party. Then you can tell us about it."

The teacher eagerly listened to the very creative ideas that the students discussed with much energy. Each pair of students then told the entire class about their birthday party plans. These activities took twenty minutes, which meant five minutes more than had been planned, but the teacher knew that the time was being used well.

"Good work. Those are very creative ideas. Now, let's get back to our desks. We'll take this one step further. Of course, in this English class we will write often, including today. In a few months our school will celebrate its twenty-fifth birthday. Take the next five minutes and write your ideas about what would be the perfect birthday party and celebration for our school. You could list some ideas, but also include at least one paragraph where you describe your most important idea.

"After you finish writing, everyone will read the school birthday ideas out loud. We will then revise our papers tomorrow and share them with the principal. Maybe some of our ideas will actually become part of the school's birthday celebration. Now, begin thinking and writing. If you have any questions, let me know as I move around the classroom."

Which of those two getting-acquainted approaches would be more productive? Which would be more revealing? Which would be more effective with middle school students? Which approach is more consistent with the unique characteristics of middle school students? Is there some merit to each of these approaches or not? Which approach could help more as middle school students take some important yet cautious and guided steps at the start of a school year through part of the middle school maze?

The subject of middle school teaching and teachers must include the reality that teaching well is very demanding, exhausting, draining work, while it is also fascinating, meaningful, and rewarding. There are teaching moments of joy and teaching moments of despair. The typical middle school day includes very little time for teachers to trade ideas, to share concerns, to solve problems together, to encourage each other, or to advise and counsel each other unless that time is intentionally scheduled for teaching teams to meet or unless educators make such interaction happen otherwise.

Before we consider some teaching methods that work and before we contrast those methods with much less effective teaching techniques, it can be beneficial to hear from some teachers. Does the reader identify with any of the following voices of teachers? Can the reader see any of himself or herself—now, in the past, or potentially in the future—in any of these portraits?

"How was my summer? To be honest, it was not the best. Oh, we took a few short trips that our children loved—the beach, an amusement park, plus Washington, D.C. We cooked out a lot on the grill and we enjoyed our new deck. But I kept thinking about this new school year and that was so discouraging. I have 7th grade math classes this year. I've taught 8th grade science forever, but nobody else is certified to teach math, so I got stuck with that and instead of hiring somebody new for math they hired somebody new for my old job. I can take the hint. So my attitude about this year is sour." Emily Fisher was being honest about her attitude, but her friend could sense trouble.

Katie Bell had taught with Emily on an 8th grade teaching team for many years. Katie tried to help. "Seventh grade math is perfect. You can use sports statistics to teach fractions and decimals. You can use money to teach percents. You can use their hobbies for word problems. The old awful 'two trains left a station' problem becomes a 'Shawn and Thomas were skateboarding' situation. Or use other wholesome interests and talents of the students. You can have a great year."

Emily was not convinced. "Years ago I taught 8th grade math. I really prefer 8th graders. As for subject, I really prefer science. In college I majored in biology. Math was my minor. Then I got a master's degree with an emphasis on biology and on earning certification to teach. I've been teaching for nineteen years. I can retire in eleven years. I cannot change jobs and start over somewhere else. I have to do everything all over again for a different grade and a different subject. I had science down to a, well, science. It could take hours every day to prepare for math classes. And 7th graders are not like 8th graders. I really prefer the oldest middle school students. This year looks awful."

There was more on Emily's complaint list. "The only solution I can come up with is to use the materials the math department has instead of creating my own lessons. We have that set of one hundred "Magic Math Mania" lesson plans. There are workbooks for the students and plenty of prepared quizzes, tests, plus math videos. There are some good math Web sites we can use. So my plan is to just go by the book this year. I intend to arrive at school the last minute allowed and leave at the earliest minute allowed. The machine will grade our quizzes and tests.

"I hate to become that type of teacher, but I'm frustrated. I have not been treated fairly. I'll do the job in a way that meets all requirements, so nobody can evaluate me as not complying. How's that for showing the system they treated me wrong?"

Katie was concerned for her friend and for the 7th grade students Emily would teach. "Emily, I hope this will work out. It is the only chance your students will have to learn 7th grade math. Who knows, maybe next year you'll be back to teaching 8th grade? That means you would be preparing the students you could teach next year while you teach them this year."

Emily had more to complain about. "I doubt that will happen. The people who run this place tell us to get to know the students, but those administrators never treat us the way we are supposed to treat the students. Get to know the students, they tell us. Establish a relationship with the students. Well, nobody in charge here established any relationship with me. If they had done that, they would know that I prefer 8th grade science. The principal and the assistant principal never asked me about that. They just called me in one day and said this is the way it is going to be. Is that any way to reward loyalty?

"I've been at this school for nineteen years. I've seen principals and assistant principals come and go, but I'm one of the loyal teachers who keep this place on a firm foundation. If all of the teachers left as often as the school administrators of this place left, well, the school would fall apart."

Emily paused, but she was not finished. "And something else. Could you believe that awful professional development program we had to sit through yesterday? The only professional part was that the guest speaker got paid, but it was way too much money for doing way too little work. We hear that same old speech every few years; students don't care how much you know until they know how much you care. Wait a minute. Don't the students have the responsibility to behave and to work? Why do schools tell us that if any student is below average it is our fault? If they sleep in class and never turn in homework, it is their fault.

"That speaker went on for six hours making us do those little tasks and watch those corny and contrived videos. Then she collected her money, packed up her supplies, and took her show to the next school, which she knows nothing about.

"We would get more done if we used those six hours to work with each other on lessons to use in our classrooms. But no, the principal planned for that guest speaker and now the school board can be told that we were trained in all the social engineering politically correct stuff we have to listen to year after year.

"I'm really frustrated by all of this. I'm sorry to take your time with my complaints, but you know what I mean. I have heard a few other teachers complain about what they have to teach this year and I heard a lot of exasperation at that pointless development program. Oh well, school starts tomorrow. Maybe I can get those math materials arranged and copies made for the first week. What are you doing today after our faculty meeting?"

Katie was enthusiastic in her answer. "I'm going to meet with all of the new teachers. I was asked to help set up a mentor program for them. Then I'll finish setting up my classroom, but I did most of that last week, and I have a meeting with a family and a school counselor to learn about a new student who is super-gifted and talented academically, but he was homeschooled last year. We just want his transition back into public school to go well. Lots to do."

Emily knew it was time for the faculty meeting. "Well, have a good day, at least what is left of it after this meeting. These faculty meetings last too long. We have better uses of our time. I sure hope the copy machines work today. They break so often. I need to make a lot of copies of math materials for 7th graders."

Somewhere between "This is your job this year, so do it" and "You pick whatever schedule of classes you would like to teach" is a reasonable, realistic approach that merges the school's master schedule with the experiences, the talents, the strengths, and the goals of teachers. Changes in teaching assignments can be made through a professional and humane process that involves input, listening, and give-and-take, plus consideration of all factors.

Middle school teachers who truly grasp the middle school concept will eagerly get to know the students and their strengths. Middle school administrators who truly grasp the importance of leading by example will treat teachers, whenever possible and proper, the way they want teachers to treat students—build a relationship, play to strengths, listen, provide support, seek and use input, maintain open communication, be aware.

The experience that middle school students will have is shaped at school more by teachers than by anyone else at school. The way school administrators work with teachers can, in some very important and effective ways, set examples for how the students are to be treated. What could middle school administrators do to prevent or to reverse Emily Fisher's attitude about the new school year?

What could middle school administrators do to help inspire more attitudes like the one that follows in this story about Mark Lucas, a middle school science teacher?

"I can't wait. Really, I cannot wait. This summer my wife and I took our children to many museums and interactive science exhibitions and to historical sites. All of us learned so much. My son is thirteen and he is really eager to be an 8th grader. My daughter is eleven and she has all the excitement plus the apprehension of most new 6th graders. Both of them love to learn.

"I watched them at the places we visited this summer. They always paid attention. They asked questions. They had very creative ideas. They keep asking when we will go to more museums and science exhibitions or historical places. Why wait until next summer for them or for my students, I thought? Why not make my science classroom a continuous interactive adventure?" Mark Lucas was obviously very excited about the new school year that would begin the next day.

John Matthews was not convinced that the new school year deserved any excitement. "Mark, dream on. What you and your wife can accomplish with your wonderful children at those places you visited is not going to be the same as what you can accomplish in your crowded classroom with twenty-nine twelve-year-old 7th graders who have no interest in science. You are in for a disappointment. Come on, you've taught middle school science for fifteen years or so. You're a great teacher, but taking your children to a fancy interactive science park or museum is different from teaching six classes of 7th grade science at this school every day."

Mark had a quick and a certain reply to his friend. "Goodness, John, when did you give up? You are the last person I would expect to say anything discouraging. Your students always do great work. You are known for your energy and your enthusiasm. The 8th graders who have you for math are so ready for high school math that they win high school awards and then college scholarships. What happened to you?"

John was honest. "For the past three years I've been trying to become a middle school assistant principal. I have had three interviews, but no results. There was one opening this summer and the principal at that school never interviewed me, never returned my phone calls, and never answered my e-mails. It is so frustrating. I'm better qualified than the people who have been chosen for those jobs I tried to get.

"So, I'm frustrated with it all. I'll do my job well. I always do. But it's discouraging to work hard, put in all those extra hours and, you know as well as I do, it is not noticed or appreciated. Why should I work so hard if this school district is not working hard for me?"

Mark had an answer, but he knew that his friend needed more than a few tried and true pep talk phrases. "Well, John, let's do this. You come visit my classroom next week. What I intend to do with very interactive science you can do with interactive math. I've got a baseball activity coming up. There is so much science in hitting a baseball. You could use baseball statistics to do all kinds of math problems and to teach math skills. Maybe we can do this together and get noticed by the big officials in the school district. If more of them notice your work, it might help you become an assistant principal next year."

John was not convinced, but he was not defeated yet, either. "OK. We'll try that. I'm going to give this school district one more year and if I'm not an assistant principal by early next summer, I'll apply to other school districts and get it done that way. I've been loyal and dedicated, but I have to advance my career. Thanks for listening and thanks for the baseball idea. It will work. It's perfect for middle school students.

"Maybe I'll bring in some old baseball cards and use the statistics from them. We could make new, modern baseball cards or some other kind of math card. Then I can take those to my next interview and show how well I work with middle school students. Maybe we could present this at a faculty meeting and then I could tell the interview committee how well I work with teachers. I'm still frustrated, but I can't let that keep me from giving this year's students the best I can give them."

What could a middle school principal or assistant principal do to support John's administrative ambitions while still holding him responsible for the superior teaching he is known for? Perhaps a substitute teacher could teach John's classes one day while John shadows the school administrators and gets an introduction to the real minute-to-minute work of a principal or of an assistant principal. Maybe John could be the chair of a committee that seriously studies ways to improve the school. John could make a presentation to the faculty about his teaching methods. Aware administrators could help reduce John's frustration, build his administrative readiness, and help prepare a future leader for the school district.

Dear Ellen,

I need your advice, please. I could have called or e-mailed, but making myself put these thoughts on paper just seems right. I really need your advice. You've been in education forever and you have more enthusiasm for school than people who are much younger than you are. You and I have known each other since college. I remember our discussion about becoming great teachers. I was a great teacher. I'm not great now. You have been better than great as a teacher and as a middle school administrator. How do you stay so energetic and so confident and so optimistic?

We've both been in this work for twenty-eight years. We could retire in two years. Ellen, this is the eighth day of school and I am thinking over and over that there are 172 days to go. I have never thought that way about a school year. I remember when I took off eight years to have children and stay with them until the younger child started kindergarten. I was so glad to teach my 6th graders again. Not anymore.

I'm fifty-eight years old. The students I teach are eleven or twelve years old. Suddenly I feel like a great-grandparent. I'm too old and too out of touch. They need a teacher who is twenty-three years old, just finished college, knows all about technology, and will wake up each morning eager to spend the day with eleven-year-olds who are so determined to make sense out of middle school even though it seems to be the biggest place they have ever been.

I used to be able to fascinate the students. My classroom was alive. That's changed. I used to love the energy and the curiosity of the students. Now, their curiosity takes us off the subject I have to teach that day. Their energy is perfect for physical education class, but not for my English class.

I need your advice. How do I connect with these children? How do I learn all these new technology ways to teach or can I just keep using my old-fashioned ways? How do I keep from becoming the teacher who creates busy work for the students so I just ride out my last years until retirement?

I really hate this attitude of mine, but it's real and it won't go away easily. I have to teach for two more years to fully qualify for retirement. It bothers me that these could be my worst years ever as a teacher. The students deserve better. What should I do?

Martha

Dear Martha,

Well, I was a middle school counselor for three years before I became an assistant principal and then a principal, so let me put my counselor experience to work.

Don't undervalue your old-fashioned teaching methods. Technology can do some good, but it has limits. Some teaching technology is just old-fashioned materials put on a screen and some is really new stuff, but new and electronic cannot guarantee better. What you can accomplish working face-to-face with a 6th grader is more than what any technology gadget can accomplish working screen-to-face with the same student. The computer cannot like, personally encourage, listen to, inspire, or care about the student. You have always done all of that, so keep doing it.

The truth is our work does get more difficult, more complicated, and more demanding every year. We are told every year to do more. We are told every year to do the impossible. We are told to do for students what no other people in our society are told or are expected to do. It is hard work, but we are the people who signed up for this work.

It is important to take good care of yourself. Teaching is exhausting. Protect the health of your heart, mind, body, and soul. Our employer is not going to do that for us. You have to do that for yourself. Shift gears on the weekend. Keep singing in the church choir that means so much to you. Spend time with that newborn granddaughter. You and your husband like to play golf so keep doing that. Put in the time and effort it takes to be an excellent teacher. Put in the time and effort to enjoy being an excellent person, to have meaningful family experiences daily, and to savor the goodness of life itself.

One other thing. You really are an excellent teacher and I hope you know that. I was told years ago that the best teachers are never satisfied with their work or with their results. That is part of what makes great teachers great; they continually increase their standards and they continually increase the measures of success. You are one of those great teachers, otherwise you would just accept things the way they are. Begin each day anew with your students. Let your energy and vitality and creativity combine with their curiosity and vigor. I'll try to find a way to visit your school and your classroom. I'll see great teaching. If having me come again after that or if talking to me is helpful, consider it done.

Ellen

The middle school principal or assistant principal who daily remembers that the essential work at school is done in classrooms will daily do everything possible to work with teachers knowing that he or she is simultaneously working for students. The next chapter will concentrate on the administration of a middle school, but the stories above plant some ideas and topics, which will be detailed in the next chapter.

The teachers in the preceding stories present genuine concerns and authentic encouragement. Teaching well is exhausting. Teaching middle school well can be extra-exhausting. Great middle school teachers get to know their students. Great middle school teachers also get to know themselves very well. This self-knowledge includes being very aware of changes in energy level, enthusiasm, commitment, attitude, or physical health.

Taking great care of students and of their education should not be done in ways that cause a teacher to take bad care of himself or herself. Colleagues can be sources of encouragement and guidance. Family and friends can be key support systems. There are ups and downs during a school year for teachers as there are ups and downs throughout a teaching career. Take good care of heart, mind, body, and soul so you can thrive with the a-maze-ing middle school students you teach.

Now that we have reminded middle school teachers about the high importance of taking great care of themselves and now that we have reminded middle school administrators about the realistic toll that teaching well can impose on the best of teachers, we return to the good news that middle school is fertile ground for educational entrepreneurs.

Worksheets are misnamed. When worksheets are distributed to middle school students who then silently fill in blanks on the sheet for eight minutes, it may appear as if work is being done, but that is misleading. "Worksheeting" is not teaching. Worksheets do not cause learning. Worksheets do not connect with or build on the unique characteristics of middle school students. Worksheets are contradictory with the unique characteristics of middle school students. Evaluate the following examples.

"For the next eight minutes you will work silently on your own to do this worksheet. Do your own work. Do not use any notes or the textbook. Read each of the eight sentences on the worksheet. Find the spelling error in each sentence and correct it. Find the grammar error in each sentence and correct that. Depending on the results we may move on to our next activity or we may have to do this worksheet over again." The teacher moved throughout the classroom to be sure everyone worked, or to be more accurate, to be sure everyone worksheeted.

* * *

"There are twenty-seven students in this class. We have some spelling work to do and some grammar work to do. We will divide into three groups of nine students. I'll give each group nine cards. On each card is a word. Each group will take their nine words and put them in the best order to create a proper sentence. None of the words are capitalized, so just imagine that the word your group picks to begin the sentence begins with a capital letter. When you have the words arranged into a sentence, I'll give you another card with a period on one side and a question mark on the other. You will decide which to use. Any questions about what you are to do? Everyone participates. Each group will line up according to who holds the card for the first word in the sentence on through the person who holds the last card with the final word and the punctuation. Looks as if we are ready. Let's start."

The teacher moved throughout the room, listening to the nine students decide together in each group how to arrange the words. The teacher offered some guidance and encouragement, but the students made their decisions together. One group realized that their words could be arranged in more than one logical sequence. The teacher made a mental note to discuss with the students how lively and how creative writing could become just by moving words around.

If the eight-minute worksheet is a generic, prepackaged page that the teacher made copies of and used because the class is reading chapter 3 and this is worksheet 3:1, the results will be very limited. The person who wrote the textbook and the worksheet does not know the students in classroom 221 who are working on 6th grade spelling and grammar.

If the teacher created the worksheet, included some misspellings that her students had actually made recently, included vocabulary the students needed to learn, and used sentences that were real, the result can be that important learning would occur. An example is "Were will the sixth grade chess club hold there meeting this Friday!" For a teacher who needs students to realize the spelling difference between *were* or *where*, between *there* or *their* or *they're*, this sentence can be effective. For 6th graders who participate in the chess club, this sentence gets extra notice. Real sentences that connect with the real lives of students are more effective than generic sentences that fill the ordinary worksheet.

The 6th graders who participated in the three groups of nine students had to think, had to listen, had to decide, got to move around some, and got to be interactive. The teacher may need these students to complete a custom-made sheet of sentences prepared by the teacher for those students. Doing this after their groups present the three sentences will build upon and apply what has been learned because students will be prepared for that and the variety of activity will enhance the overall result.

Perhaps it would be reasonable to consider putting up signs in middle school classrooms proclaiming, "You have entered a worksheet-free zone," "You are in a think-and-learn zone," and "In this room, we cause learning."

If such signs seem unusual, go into a middle school locker room and check for signs or posters about athletics. "There is no I in team" or "Quitters never win, winners never quit" could be on locker room signs. If coaches can communicate aphorisms to athletes via signs, what prevents a teacher from communicating via classroom signs?

The teacher who uses the three groups of nine students to assemble sentences is using an active, creative, interactive teaching method. Those twenty-seven students could then be given a sheet of paper that the teacher prepared with five groups of twelve words per group. Each student arranges each group of words into a proper sentence and adds the necessary punctuation. The first activity incorporated movement, thinking, interaction, decision-making, and learning within an overall creative process that had a clearly explained, designed procedure and desired result.

The second activity had no movement, but did require thinking and decision-making that led to learning in a structured process. Creativity and structure can be simultaneous. Creativity is not the enemy of structure and structure is not the enemy of creativity. The middle school teacher who uses both is wisely applying the reality that middle school students can thrive in an atmosphere of creativity, yet need to have the guidance and the boundaries that structure provides.

The instructional results from the two activities—groups creating sentences followed by each student forming sentences from words provided on a custom-designed paper—will very likely surpass the results from the generic worksheet even if the generic worksheet is repeated.

In addition to more and better student achievement, there is another benefit. The teacher who distributes generic worksheet after generic worksheet is forcing himself or herself into a generic career. The teacher who uses a variety of creativity and structure, of group interaction and of individual work, and who adjusts instruction to meet the learning needs of today's students while causing the intended learning of today's curriculum, will have a more productive and meaningful career.

Speaking of today's students, it is possible that instructional activities that worked today will not work tomorrow with the same students at the same middle school. How is that possible? The human variable is at work. The survey responses mentioned flexibility and the wise, realistic, aware middle school teacher is as flexible as necessary to cause the intended learning. "But that activity we did yesterday worked so well. I tried a similar version today and nothing happened. What went wrong?"

Perhaps nothing went wrong that could have been predicted. Recall that two middle school students who are best friends today could be major enemies tomorrow and then friends again in a few more days. Middle school students are known to sometimes shift from extreme to extreme. "I hate math class" can change in a few days to "We did the neatest stuff in math class today. It was money math and I got a 98% on the quiz we took."

The "I hate math class" comment may have been due to a low math test score. With a grade of 98% math is liked again. The next grade in math may determine a middle school student's temporary love or hate of math. For similar reasons, the math instructional activity that worked yesterday may not work today or tomorrow.

If a middle school class lasts for one hour, it can be very age-effective to include three or four different activities that each last for fifteen or twenty minutes. "Sit still and read chapter 8 silently until the bell rings" is a directive that may appear to have merit—chapter 8 needs to be read—yet there are age-effective ways to accomplish this that apply and build upon the characteristics of middle school students.

Chapter 8 has three short sections in it. One section could be read aloud by various students. One section could be outlined by each student individually. The teacher and three students who are very interested in speech, drama, and theater could take turns reading the third section aloud. Each student could write a summary of sections 1 and 3 to go along with the outline of section 2. Then the teacher and the students could list the major facts from the chapter and analyze the most significant ideas from the chapter. With that process, students are reading, listening, writing, participating, thinking, and engaging.

Yes, students need to be able to sit down and read a chapter, but is the greater goal to silently and without pause read the chapter from start to finish or is the greater goal to learn, understand, analyze, and know the content of the chapter? Of course, the reading technique that works today may not work tomorrow, so the well-prepared middle school teacher has a collection of reading methods, activities, and projects that can be interchanged as needed.

Making adjustments to address today's new reality is part of the middle school teaching adventure that energizes some teachers, yet frustrates and discourages other teachers. Such adjustments are necessary and are realistic. Master them rather than condemn them. Middle school teaching is not a static endeavor. Middle school teaching at its best and at its essence is dynamic because, among many reasons, the middle school maze is ever-changing and the middle school students journeying through the maze are dynamic people in a dynamic process.

It is excessive and pessimistic to observe that middle school is the last chance students have to correct misbehaviors and to correct bad academic habits, tendencies, or performance. It is not excessive or overly optimistic to observe that there is a better chance of a student reversing misbehavior and/or academic inadequacy in middle school than for that reversal to occur after middle school. One reason for a higher likelihood of middle school results is the teaching team organization within a middle school. The teaching team design can be the foundation, the heart, the soul of a middle school.

The 8th grade Titan team at Jackson Middle School has six teachers and 144 students. The teachers each have six classes to teach daily with twenty-two to twenty-eight students per class. The classes taught are math, science, English, social studies, reading, and Spanish. The students rotate through the classes daily. Each teacher on the team teaches every student on the team every day. The team has a planning period daily to meet together and a separate planning period to work individually. During those two planning periods, the students on the Titan team are in elective classes including computer applications, Latin, health, physical education, art, theater, vocal music, band, orchestra, technology education, or industrial arts.

When these students are in high school they will not rotate through a group of six teachers who collectively teach the same students daily and meet as a team daily. Class schedules for high school students can vary so much that perhaps no two students have the same schedule with the same teachers for the entire school day. High schools usually have larger enrollments than middle schools.

The last opportunity many students will have for the thorough, collective, unified benefits of a teaching team that knows the student quite well is in middle school. That reality increases the importance of and the responsibility of the middle school teaching team. The following discussion is during a meeting of the six teachers on the Titan team. Please notice what the teaching team's organization and daily planning period enables the teachers to achieve.

Teacher 1: It's the team leader's job to get us started, so let's start. Our first topic is class schedules. Does anyone see a need to move a student out of a class or into a class for any reason?

Teacher 2: Thomas Anderson and Jennifer Rodriquez are in my 1st period math class. They can do algebra and I would like to see them move into my 2nd period algebra class. They both have reading class second period, so I hope that switch works. If not, they could move to my 5th period algebra class. They each have science 5th period now.

Teacher 3: My 2nd period reading class is a little big, so if two students move to 1st period that helps balance things some. Thomas and Jennifer are good readers. The 2nd period class is average to good readers, so they could make that transition to 1st period which is good to very good readers. It would mean more of a math challenge for them and more of a reading challenge, but they are both quite capable of doing the work well. I would be glad to call their families and explain what we are doing for these students.

Teacher 4: I hope that plan works. I would like to see them stay in the 5th period science class. They are both great science students and in 5th period we actually do some high school level chemistry and biology work. It is the most challenging science class and every student in it asked for it because they really like science and they have a career goal that requires a lot of science.

Teacher 1: That works. Please call both families when we finish this meeting and then talk to Thomas and Jennifer. I will let the counselors know to change the schedules in the computer system, but I'll wait on that until you have talked to the families and to the students. Are there any other schedule changes to consider?

Teacher 5: I've mentioned my 8th period English class before. They have reading 7th period and then they come to me for English. Most of them are two grade levels behind in reading. A few are three or four grade levels behind. I've wondered if we could make some changes somehow so I could work closely with the students who are three or four grade levels behind and still help the students who are two grade levels behind.

Teacher 6: I think we could do a lot to help with that. Tell me who you are most concerned about and I can work with them on reading in social studies class. Our librarian is a reading expert. Maybe once or twice a week she could work with part of your class 8th period. Maybe your English class 8th period could become a second reading class until they all move up a grade level or two in reading. They need the English work, but they have to catch up in reading or school is just not going to work very well for them.

Teacher 5: Good ideas. I'd like to try them all. Let's create a big reading emphasis in my 8th period English class to build on what they do in their 7th period reading class. The librarian has offered to help us before, so I'll talk with her, and we can find some reading and English and social studies work that could blend those subjects together so we work on reading in all of those classes for this group of students while we still do some other social studies and English work too.

Teacher 1: That sounds good; I'll keep the principal informed. He might be able to get the school district's reading expert to come to the 7th period reading class or 8th period English class, or both, or help work closely with students. I'll ask our technology director if she has some reading resources that could help. Maybe seeing it on a screen could help or there could be a reading tutorial the students could do on the computer.

One other topic. We talked about adding a geometry class for the second semester. Some of the 8th graders in algebra class have moved at a fast pace and are ready for the next step. This would involve a lot of schedule changes. We have two algebra classes on our team. About half of them are ready to move into geometry and algebra is just right for the others. Let's look at a list tomorrow of those two groups and start thinking of the ripple effect through the schedule. It would be great to do this because those gifted math students deserve this opportunity. We just have to find a way to get the overall schedule to work.

Oh, yeah, we need to plan next month's team lunch event. The students loved the picnic we had last month. Next Friday we have pizza and the baked potato bar coming up. Tomorrow, let's plan the lunch event for next month. The students love those long lunch times and the special meals. Ask your 8th period classes today for ideas and let's see what they suggest. We'll get that organized tomorrow. Thanks for a good meeting. Now we each have a survey to fill out for the principal, so let's do that. It's due later today.

The six teachers on the Titan's team know the 144 students on that team very well, as individual students, as groups of twenty-five or so in a classroom, and as 144 middle-schoolers whom they work with every day. What those six teachers know about those 144 students surpasses what any standardized test can reveal. These teachers know on a daily basis and on an individual basis how students are doing. These teachers can exchange thoughts, ideas, concerns, challenges, and successes daily in their team meeting. They can quickly confront a problem and they can quickly act upon or create an opportunity. They can organize events that students will anticipate eagerly and participate in enthusiastically. The teaching teams can be the pulse, the energy, the heart, and the soul of a middle school.

A properly functioning, fully aware, conscientious, and entrepreneurial middle school teaching team can provide the learning experiences that students need today and make the necessary changes so those students get the learning experiences they need tomorrow. This same teaching team is also giving itself meaningful, rewarding, vibrant career experiences.

The teaching team meeting is not a time to allocate and copy worksheets to be used in all classes tomorrow. The team meeting is a time, place, and experience that adds to the direction that these teachers can provide to students who are navigating the middle school maze.

This chapter concludes with two activities that an 8th grade U.S. history teacher could use to help students memorize the Preamble to the U.S. Constitution. Both activities could be justified, but evaluate them in terms of which is more likely to get the desired results with and for middle school students.

Today we will begin working on memorizing the Preamble to the U.S. Constitution. The words and the ideas of the Preamble are so important that we need to memorize the words so we can better understand the ideas. Everyone is being given a copy of the Preamble right now. You are also being given ten pieces of paper that are about the size of an index card. On each of your ten pieces of paper write part of the Preamble. For example, on one side you could write, "We the people of the United States" and on the other side write the number one since that is the first group of words in the Preamble. If you think a hint would help, you may write the number one and then the word "We" next to it so you know that the first group of words begins with "We." Let's take about eight minutes for everyone to make their set of Preamble flash cards, then you can begin to memorize each of the ten parts until you know the complete Preamble.

* * *

Today we are going to sing, maybe dance, we might cheer some, we will write, and we will memorize. It's all about U.S. history so first I'll show you a short video of a very talented singer performing the National Anthem. The video

Chapter 3

also shows a sign language interpreter communicating the words of "The Star-Spangled Banner." The video also shows a group of dancers whose patriotic costumes and choreography add even more meaning to the singing and to the signing of the National Anthem.

Now, we are going to put music and dance and other creativity into the Preamble of the U.S. Constitution. I am passing out a copy of the Preamble to everyone. It's typed so you have lots of room on the page to write ideas about how certain phrases could be supported with music and dance. I know you've been working on dance this year in your art class and vocal music class, so you should be experts.

First, we need to know the words to the Preamble. I made twenty-five signs, one sign for everyone. Each sign has a word or a few words of the Preamble on it. Your first job is to arrange yourselves in order around the desks so the signs are in the right sequence to form the Preamble. One at a time, starting with Andrea, hold up your sign so everyone can get familiar with the words even though the words are not in order yet. Good, we have now seen each sign. Now, start with David, read the words on your sign out loud so everyone hears the words. Good. We are ready.

The next thing to do is to arrange yourselves into the proper sequence to form the Preamble to the U.S. Constitution. Of course, you may give each other ideas and directions, but be polite, friendly, and just talk at normal conversation level without being loud. Ready. Go.

After a few minutes, the students had completed the task. The teacher then said, "Good work. Now keep standing up in that sequence. We are all going to say the Preamble together. Good. Now, Joey, Samantha, and Drew, set your cards down. Now we will all say the Preamble with only twenty-two of the cards left for us to see. Good. Now, Annie, Jared, Martha, Margaret, Blaine, Upton, and Beverly, put your signs down. Now we all say the Preamble with fifteen of the cards left for us to see. Good, now, who knows the Preamble? Great, several hands went up. Now, everyone put your cards down. Allison, you raised your hand quickly, so you go first. Great job, Allison. Let's hear from more Preamble scholars."

After eight students volunteered to recite the Preamble alone, the other seventeen students were put in groups of three or four with one or two of the eight who had recited the Preamble. Each group worked together to be sure everyone memorized the Preamble. Each group also was told to add some movement or clapping or dance to add to their presentation. By the end of the presentations, every student knew the Preamble. To be sure the work had been mastered, the teacher had each student silently and on their own write the Preamble word for word.

Which of those two instructional activities would be more likely to result in the desired goal for each student in this 8th grade U.S. history class to memorize the words of the Preamble? Which of those two instructional activities prepares students better for tomorrow's lesson, which is to analyze the ideas and concepts of the Preamble of the U.S. Constitution? Which of those two instructional activities is more age-effective for thirteen-year-old 8th graders? Which of those instructional activities gives the students a better learning experience and gives the teacher a more rewarding teaching experience?

Of course, not every class period can sing, dance, cheer, clap, and move around to arrange signs. Yes, there are times when pencil-and-paper work has to be done silently and individually by each student sitting at his or her desk. Yet, the eleven- to fourteen-year-olds in middle schools are likely to learn and to thrive when middle school teachers tap into their inner educational entrepreneur and create age-effective instruction for students based on what their teacher knows in general about the characteristics of middle school students and what the teacher knows in particular about the uniqueness of each student who is being taught now.

A teacher's impact is almost completely within his or her classroom. Teachers can trade ideas in a team meeting and impact what happens throughout that teaching team. Teachers could offer ideas at a faculty meeting that may have impact throughout the school. Still, most of the impact that a teacher has will be and should be in the classroom.

School administrators—principals and assistant principals—work in a school but have vastly different job descriptions than do teachers. School administrators and teachers work in the same building, but their jobs are quite different. When the school administration and the teachers have the same goals for and the same ideal of a middle school, the working relationship can be more harmonious and the results can be superior. With such thoughts in mind, the next chapter will deal with the administration of a middle school.

Chapter Four

The Administration of a Middle School

The last chapter emphasized that for teachers who are educational entrepreneurs, middle school is fertile ground. These teachers apply, build upon, and guide the unique characteristics of middle school students to cause the intended learning through a wide variety of creative, structured, energetic, challenging, age-effective instructional activities.

There is similar good news for middle school principals and assistant principals. Middle school is fertile ground for entrepreneurial executives who will (A) lead and manage in ways that encourage and support teachers to be educational entrepreneurs, (B) provide an atmosphere, setting, climate, and day-to-day operations that apply, build upon, and guide the unique characteristics of middle school students, and (C) work directly with students to lead and to manage them in age-effective ways.

The uniqueness of middle school calls for some particular approaches to administration. Principals and assistant principals at elementary schools, middle schools, and high schools face some shared problems and opportunities, but each level of schooling calls for specific methods and actions of leadership and management. Middle school administration that works well is uniquely tailored for the reality of and the possibilities of middle school.

The survey question that relates to middle school leadership and management asked, "What must middle school principals and assistant principals know and do that is unique to middle schools?" Some ideas and insights from the survey about what middle school administrators must know are below. The second group of quotations is about what administrators must do.

- "Know that the brains of students are not fully developed. The students are not mini-adults."

- "Know the middle school team philosophy and the middle school curriculum."
- "Administrators must know that teachers and staff have families and other outside interests. School is not necessarily their lives; it is their job."
- "Know that the students are sophisticated enough to identify structural and procedural flaws."
- "Know that students want boundaries and that students crave kindness."
- "Know that they are dealing with students who have drastic emotional and physical changes."
- "Know the research and the best practices related to the age group."
- "Know that no two hours on the job will be the same. We have to discipline, compliment, supervise, listen, and advise all at the same time."
- "Know how to get the absolute best out of students and teachers."
- "Know the challenges that families and students in their school face."
- "Know about the mental and emotional development of middle school students."
- "Know that everyone wants praise and to feel special. Know that this is a critical time in the life of a student."
- "Know that students are questioning authority more."

Some survey responses about what middle school administrators must do are below.

- "Treat each student with respect."
- "Implement a wide curriculum for all students, communicate with parents, teachers, and students, connect with students."
- "Administrators need to treat staff as professionals. Advise them and give them a chance to improve. Too many times, new teachers are dismissed if it appears their group of students will negatively affect the test scores of the school."
- "Educate the teachers about the pitfalls of power struggles, of having the last word with students. Use unconventional approaches to address at-risk students who do not fear authority. Develop relationships with the faculty and students."
- "Lay down ground rules early and be consistent."
- "Show guidance. This age group of students needs to see examples of respect to guide them."
- "Be committed to this age group and to the research about and best practices for this age group."
- "Bring in staff members who can relate to multiple cultures and various ethnicities. Help teachers realize that a teacher can learn what to teach, but a terrible relationship with students will tear all the good apart."
- "Take the time to build relationships."

- "Do what it takes to provide services—transportation, counseling, child care, continuing education, medical, mental health—and resources to handle the situations that schools and teachers are increasingly asked to deal with daily."
- "Have a safe and orderly environment."
- "Be consistent with staff, students, and parents."

Does a middle school administrator have to be a super-human to know all that needs to be known and to do all that needs to be done? No, super-human status is not required, but ordinary status is not sufficient either.

The teacher who thrives in middle school knows the reality, the wonder, the challenge, the possibilities of working with eleven- to fourteen-year-old students. The school administrator who thrives in middle school knows the reality, the wonder, the challenge, the possibilities of working with eleven- to fourteen-year-old students and the accompanying reality, wonder, challenge, and possibilities of working with the faculty and staff who work with those students, plus working with the parents and guardians of middle school students.

Middle school administration is not for everyone, yet if you are right for it and if it is right for you, the result can be superior. Let's explore how these results can be obtained.

Middle school teachers who are most effective with middle school students combine the professional responsibility of being in charge with the power of the personal connection tailored to the uniqueness of eleven- to fourteen-year-old students. That teacher knows that what must happen—learning—is promoted by a variety of age-effective teaching activities, enthusiasm, challenging academics, and application of what is being learned to the wholesome knowledge, talents, and interests of the students. The astute middle school teacher knows that how 6th, 7th, and 8th grade learning is caused relates to productive instruction and to partnership-building connections in the classroom so students commit to the teacher and to learning.

Ideally, students would comply, cooperate, work, behave, study, and learn because they are supposed to do that and because they are supposed to obey the teacher. For a variety of reasons, such automatic compliance is increasingly not the norm in the current reality of school life, yet great results can still be obtained. Those results do not effortlessly come to a teacher. Those results come when a middle school teacher does what matters most for and what works best with today's middle school students.

The effective middle school administrator is leading and managing an organization that is filled with 6th, 7th, and 8th graders whose unique characteristics create an environment that calls for a combination of professional responsibility to be in charge plus a personal approach to dealing with students, faculty, and staff.

Middle school principals and assistant principals must know applicable education laws, regulations, and policies and must enforce them. Simultaneously, middle school administrators must know applicable and proven leadership, management, relationship-building, interpersonal communication methods to use in the moment-to-moment real-world work of a middle school.

Community is a concept, perhaps an ideal, that middle school administrators can use as a guideline. "Am I working with students, teachers, and staff in ways that increase student achievement while building commitments in our school between students, teachers, and staff?" is a good question for middle school administrators to ask themselves often.

A person who is the principal of a middle school will benefit from not emphasizing the word "principal" at the expense of de-emphasizing the words "of a middle school." There are leadership and management truths that school administrators should apply at the elementary school, middle school, and high school levels. There are methods of leadership and management that administrators of a middle school are wise to apply in ways that administrators of elementary schools or high schools would not use or would use differently.

Consider this aphorism: "Leaders listen." All administrators of all schools need to listen to many people. How, when, where, and why a school administrator listens to middle school students can be enhanced by doing that in ways that are most instructional for and most age-effective for eleven- to fourteen-year-olds. Similarly, how, when, where, and why a school administrator listens to faculty and staff at a middle school can be enhanced by doing that in ways that are most realistic and effective in the middle school workplace for those teachers and staff members. The principal of a middle school leads and manages a unique educational community that calls for some specified leadership and management awareness, skills, understanding, and actions.

The middle school community ideally is an active place of continuous learning and of continuous relationship building. The most effective leadership is by example. The middle school principal who tells teachers at a faculty meeting, "You must get to know your students," can lead by example in many important ways including the following.

Get to know the students by being in classrooms, being in hallways, being in the cafeteria, being at school events—note: being there is not merely showing up; rather, it is active. Actively being there means interacting with people, reaching out to people, initiating conversations, talking to the student who is sitting alone.

Get to know teachers by being in their classrooms and following up those frequent, informal visits with support such as giving a social studies teacher whose topic in class was the U.S. Constitution a copy of a newspaper article about the Supreme Court. Such support is not earth-shattering, but it is genuine, it is appreciated, and when done continuously it helps build professional relationships that help strengthen the foundation of a middle school community.

In fulfilling the duty of "Leaders listen," how do middle school administrators listen differently than elementary school or high school administrators? Recall that the middle school years can be times of turbulent, volatile extremes as a student's best friend this week could be no friend at all next week. How does a middle school assistant principal listen to two 7th graders whose friendship reversed and collapsed so suddenly that it sparked rumors that led to a confrontation that disrupted a classroom and resulted in both students being sent to the office?

It will help to hear what is not said. It will help to translate "We were friends. Now I hate him," into "We were friends. Then he started liking my girlfriend. Now I am so mad at him because everything fell apart."

The adept middle school principal may hear a teacher say behind closed doors in the principal's office, "These students just won't behave. I try everything. They are incorrigible." The students' misbehavior is being reported accurately. The teacher may also be saying, "I thought I was a good teacher. It's just not working this year. I need some ideas and some guidance."

Leaders listen. Middle school leaders listen continuously, with awareness, with sensitivity, with creativity, and with responses. The response to the teacher above is not "You are so right. These students are out of control. All I work on is discipline with students that teachers kick out of class. You think it's tough in your classroom? Try being in my job."

What would be a better reply? What is the teacher communicating that goes beyond what the words above so strongly, yet incompletely, express? What could an aware middle school administrator hear, spoken or unspoken, and how could that middle school administrator best respond?

Perhaps the principal says, "When I was in your classroom a few days ago everything was great. The discussion was really scholarly. Students were participating. Students were listening. Everyone was alert and attentive. I even came back later that day and another class was as good or better. Is there a certain class that is causing problems? Did something this week suddenly change?"

That could evoke this response: "Those were great classes last week. I think something did change. A relative of a student in one of my classes got arrested a few days ago and the students in that class keep spreading rumors about it. And for some reason a lot of my students went to some concert at the Coliseum on Monday night so they were not ready for Tuesday's test. Why are they more concerned about some teenage heartthrob's concert than they are about school? Why did their parents let them stay out so late on a school night?"

Concerts happen. Some middle school students go to concerts or other late evening events on school nights. Some parents or guardians permit that. The principal wisely reminded the teacher that of the factors she can control—and 7th graders going to a Monday night concert is not one of those teacher-controlled factors—she is in full control of the instructional activities that she designs for her students.

The negative impact on learning of a 7th grader being out and up too late on a Monday night is frustrating, but it does not mean that the teacher is no longer doing a good job on Tuesday when some distracted, sleepy, and poorly prepared students are not ready for class. The aware middle school administrator listens to faculty and staff with an eagerness to fully realize what is being said, what is being implied, and what remains unspoken, but quietly and certainly expressed.

School does not happen in the principal's office or in the other administrative offices. The work done in these offices is mandatory. Records must be maintained. Meetings must be held. Conferences must be conducted. Accounting and bookkeeping must be kept accurate and up to date. The work that is done in a middle school's administrative offices by the principal, assistant principal, counselors, social worker, bookkeeper, attendance clerk, and secretaries—the titles and the number of people in these or other positions will vary by school or by school district—is work that must be done to keep the school functioning as an organization. Nonetheless, school does not happen in the principal's office or in the other administrative offices.

Most people, adults and students, at a middle school spend most of their time in classrooms. Consider a middle school of 720 students and forty faculty members for core academic classes and elective classes, plus twenty people in the administration, counseling, office staff, maintenance staff, and cafeteria staff. Six of seven hours daily are spent by students in classrooms with the other hour used for time between classes and lunch. Five of seven hours daily from when the first class starts to when the last class ends are spent by teachers in classrooms with their students. Some of the time each day by administrators will be in classrooms, but perhaps one or two hours daily among all administrators and counselors in the school is an optimistic average. The other educators and staff members probably are rarely in classrooms. What portion of the total people hours—780 people times 7 hours daily equals 5,460 hours—is spent by people in classrooms?

That is a simple calculation. 720 students times 6 hours equals 4,320. 40 teachers times 5 hours equals 200. The administrators and counselors might spend an average of one hour per day per person in classrooms. Total classroom people hours is 4,524. 4,524 divided by 5,460 equals 83 percent.

School happens in classrooms. This fact increases the importance, the urgency, the imperative that middle school administrators spend as much time as possible in classrooms to know about current instruction, to participate in instruction, and to see what students are doing. Then they can make encouraging comments to those students during lunch supervision in the cafeteria, send a written note or e-mail message to a teacher about good work, and notice concerns or problems with any teacher early so improvement and correction happen promptly.

For a middle school principal or assistant principal to work with teachers there is no replacement for spending time where teachers spend most of their time—in the classroom.

> I know that I should be in the classroom more. I need to see what the teachers and the students are doing. There's just so much to do. People stop by and insist on meeting with the principal. Two students fight and I have to deal with that. A fire alarm gets pulled. A teacher is absent and there is no substitute teacher. A bus is very late arriving to school and those students miss breakfast. Test scores arrive and they are not good enough. The school district insists that I attend some meeting about changes in how middle schools teach math. It never stops. There is so much stuff that only the principal or the assistant principal can do.
>
> I can't tell you how many times I've been in a classroom and the office calls me to come deal with some situation. There are over eight hundred students in this middle school. If 1 percent of them causes serious problems on a given day, the assistant principal and I might spend much of the day solving those problems. The other 99 percent of students deserve my time on that day, but I can't ignore those other serious problems.
>
> Yeah, I'm supposed to be the instructional leader, but I'm also the first responder to all emergencies and stuff like that. The students who cause big problems don't schedule their misbehavior around my visits to classrooms. What am I supposed to do?

Great question, which can be responded to with three questions. Does the middle school manage the principal or does the principal manage the middle school? Does the middle school lead the principal or does the principal lead the middle school? Is the principal's day consumed by reacting to situations or by "preacting" so some time-consuming, problematic situations are prevented or minimized?

How does a middle school administrator "preact" to prevent or to minimize student misbehavior? How does this administrator work with teachers so students who work hard and behave well are acknowledged properly? Or do students who refuse to work and who struggle or fail academically always get almost all of the attention? Ask for good news. That's it; just ask for good news to be reported to the principal or the assistant principal.

Teachers must write a discipline referral when students misbehave severely or when students defy discipline actions imposed by the teacher. Encourage teachers to be just as vigilant about writing good news reports.

A student makes a B on a test after failing several tests. Another student's behavior is always exemplary. A student found another student's missing purse and turned it in. Another student helped start a recycling program in the school. An 8th grade student volunteered to tutor 6th graders in math. The principal and the assistant principal who create the middle school community where more attention is given to people who do what is right than to people who misbehave are middle school administrators who are building relationships, who are leading and managing instead of merely reacting, who are acting upon the 6th, 7th, 8th graders yearning to be noticed, and who are reminding teachers that most students are cooperating most of the time.

There is often more to celebrate and to reward at a middle school than there is to lament or to punish. The celebrations and the rewards have to be done intentionally or the necessary actions involved with resolving problems and misbehavior can create the impression that nothing ever goes right.

Be there. Middle school principals and assistant principals used to be teachers. While teaching for a number of years, those future administrators made observations, evaluations, and conclusions about the principal and the assistant principal of their school. Those future administrators and/or their teaching colleagues probably wondered occasionally "Where is the principal? Where is the assistant principal? They are never in my classroom except for two quick visits each year to claim that they observed me. Don't they ever get out of the office?"

Be there. Be where teachers are. To build the middle school community in which the faculty and staff have a shared purpose that they implement through high-quality instruction and meaningful interaction with students, the middle school administrators must lead by example. This means principals and assistant principals of middle schools realize that the style of leadership and the method of management needed in a middle school are not generic leadership and management.

Leading and managing middle school teachers calls for a unique approach because those teachers, to maximize their impact, must use a unique middle school approach in their work. The middle school principal who seeks certain results in each classroom will increase the likelihood of those results by creating a school atmosphere, climate, set of procedures, and minute-to-minute standards that exemplify school-wide what is desired in each classroom.

Teachers are expected to provide compelling instructional activities that match the needs and the characteristics of middle school students. A class that uses nothing but three generic worksheets daily throughout the year is a middle school class that will painfully underperform. Middle school administrators who seek to excel cannot use the administrative equivalent of generic worksheets.

Consider a middle school principal who needs the teachers to do additional work on reading skills because the state government has established a regulation that requires each school district to confirm that every middle school student is getting more reading instruction and experience this year than they did last year. The principal is annoyed by yet another state government mandate and school district edict. The principal is frustrated for many reasons including that he and the faculty already have more than enough to do.

The principal sends the e-mail he received about the new mandate to the faculty. The original e-mail came from the central office assistant superintendent for curriculum and instruction. The principal merely added, "Please read this. We must comply. Work on this in each teaching team. Please begin this additional instruction by next Monday as the required monitoring begins then."

The teachers are likely to respond to the principal's e-mail with the same frustration and animosity that the principal had to the e-mail he received. How could a middle school principal who is thoroughly aware of and dedicated to creating a proper middle school community implement this reading mandate with the faculty effectively? The following approach provides an opportunity to see how creative, energetic leadership and people-centered management can make the most out of unexpected obstacles such as mandates or edicts.

> Welcome to our monthly faculty meeting. As you came in everyone was given a one-page reading assignment. Please take the next few minutes to read that page and then to write your one-sentence answer to the question at the bottom of the page. Then we'll hear your answers and make some decisions.

The one page reading assignment was as follows:

> Do you remember when you learned how to read? Do you remember how excited you were that now, just like your older brother, older sister, older cousin, older neighborhood friends, or older relatives, you could also read? Being able to read was something you had really wanted a lot.

During elementary school you kept learning more about reading. There were new vocabulary words to learn and then there were chapter books. You might have had a favorite author or a favorite series of books. If you got a book as a birthday present it could become your newest favorite book.

Then you got in middle school. There was reading to do, but for some reason it was not as exciting as it had been. You had other interests. The same thing happens to some, maybe many, middle school students now. They were excited about reading a few years ago, but something changed. Maybe cell phones or text messaging or video games took the place of reading and of books. Still, reading is an essential skill and our students need to read, read more, and read better.

How can we make sure that our students, all of our students, improve their reading skills and their reading eagerness? The state and the school district need us to improve reading results. We can do that. The good news is that we get to create our own program. Be creative. Be bold. Think of how working on reading can be part of what you do to help students as they learn your subject. How can we make reading a natural, normal, all-the-time way of learning? How can we make our middle school the ultimate reading place?

The teachers read the page, wrote ideas, and then shared some of their thoughts aloud after the principal said, "I really appreciate your concentration on this. We all know the importance of reading. The state and the district are asking for more results, so tell us how we can make this happen."

- "I like the idea of the entire school taking ten or fifteen minutes every day and every person in the building reads during that time. Everybody reads."
- "I'd like to see local authors come talk to the students. If the students knew more about how a book is written, they might be more interested in reading."
- "Students read all kinds of stuff on their electronic gadgets. Is there any way we can get reading for school and those electronics to work together?"
- "Let's have some reading contests. The grade that reads the most pages next month wins a pizza party. We could challenge another school to a reading competition."
- "Could we set up a 'reading buddies' program so an 8th grader who reads well helps and encourages a 6th grader who is not reading well?"
- "Let's get families involved. Parents and guardians could be asked to create a ten- or fifteen-minute reading time at home in the evening. It could be a great way to reinforce a reading time at school."
- "To be honest, I wish the state and the school district would quit sending us more mandates. They must have too much time if all they do is attend meetings and decide that we need more work to do. If they want more reading they need to give us the money they cut out of the budget for textbooks. Now that I vented, here's my idea. Let's get people to donate

books to our school. We could put some in the library and then each teaching team could have its own mini-library. Lots of people have old or even new books they never use. We could use them."

Which option is more likely to get better results from students, teachers, administrators, and the school—the e-mail or the idea-creating faculty meeting? Which option does more to build a sense of community and partnership? Which option helps build relationships? Both options deal with the same topic, which is the reading mandate. The what—reading—is not different. The how—an e-mail or an idea-generating meeting with unlimited opportunities for participation—is quite different. For middle school administrators who seek to accomplish any particular "what," much attention must be given to selecting the best "how." Dr. Earl Reum was so right when he stated, "People support what they help create."

This type of energetic leadership shown by the principal in the faculty meeting can also provide teachers with an example of how to lead in their classrooms. When an assignment can include choices and each student can select from a list of what book to read, what topic to research, what science experiment to do, or what way to present a report, the commitment can increase.

A middle school teacher spoke quite seriously to her principal about students in one class who did not turn in homework. The students were fully capable of doing the homework, but rarely did more than 50 percent of the students turn in any particular assignment. The principal had two ideas. "First, tell me the names of the students every Friday who did turn in all of the homework during that week. I'll come to the classroom on Monday to reward them. Second, experiment with choice. On Monday give them three assignments with one due on Tuesday, one due on Wednesday and one due on Thursday. Make the Wednesday and Thursday assignments longer and more difficult. Tell them they must complete two out of the three assignments. They select the two they prefer, but there is only one acceptable due date for each assignment.

"The power of choice may help. The penalty for procrastinating may have an impact if they take the time and make the effort to realize that doing the work for Tuesday is easier than doing the work for Thursday."

The results were not perfect, but they showed an improvement. Homework compliance increased the first week just because of a reward from the principal. From that point on, homework compliance was never less than 76 percent, much higher than the original 50 percent. During any week when the teacher used the three-assignment plan, compliance increased to 84 percent as the students realized more and more that working now instead of waiting a day or so was beneficial. The good results created a sense of satisfaction for the teacher and a stronger partnership between a principal and a teacher who worked together in a way that motivated students and that enhanced learning.

During an ordinary school day, middle school counselors may deal with a vast range of issues, none of which are ordinary. A neighborhood incident from the night before carries over to school the next morning and a counselor helps intervene with several students who are determined that the neighborhood feud will be the center-stage spectacle at school all day.

A vicious round of "he said/she said" rumors has four former friends divided into two pairs who are agitating and instigating rumors and threats. The counselor will provide mediation and will work with the assistant principal who will provide disciplinary action.

A student wrote comments in her English paper that alarmed the teacher, who notified the counselor. The counselor read the paper, brought the student into the office, told the principal, and called the student's family. The student's mother came to school promptly. The school's social worker helped contact two local agencies that could assist with family problems. The school counselor set up a long-term monitoring and intervention plan. The family decided to get a professional medical evaluation of their daughter.

The counselor has a weekly meeting with the seven students in the school whose separate, individual lives have been impacted recently by the death of a loved one. As needed, during the year more students join this weekly counseling session.

A car accident over the weekend resulted in serious injuries to a 7th grader who was a passenger in the car. Several students who are good friends of the injured student are very distressed about their friend. The counselor meets with these worried 6th and 7th graders.

An 8th grade teacher asked a counselor to speak in her classes about high school classes and schedules. Each presentation was about ten to fifteen minutes. Follow-up would be needed because it was quite obvious that these 8th graders had several misconceptions about high school classes and the requirements for graduation. They knew much more about high school sports and about getting a driving license than they knew about high school classes and earning a diploma.

The program for gifted and talented students is assigned to a middle school counselor for thorough evaluation and for improvement. The counselor recruits two teachers from each grade and the assistant principal to work on a plan to evaluate the services and opportunities that are provided—and that are not provided yet, but need to be added—for students who are gifted and talented.

Middle school counselors who are fully in touch with students, faculty, other colleagues, and families of students have days that move relentlessly from one issue to the next, one emergency to the next, one crisis to the next, one opportunity to the next. They work within an overall reality that in a school of seven hundred middle school students, there will always be issues, emergencies, crises, opportunities, emotions, rumors, threats, problems, progress, achievement, mediation, a sense of fulfillment, and a sense of frustration.

How can middle school administrators work best with middle school counselors? There are no secrets. There is no magic. There is no formula. There is no checklist that when completed means that no more time or effort will be required. There is the human reality that being there matters, yet that just showing up does not equal being there. Being there in an effective way requires awareness, involvement, and response.

The middle school principal or assistant principal who provides useful leadership and support for school counselors maintains a continuously updated awareness of what the counselor is working on, dealing with, concerned about and interested in starting or improving. The school's administrative team can have regular meetings to address shared concerns and to hear individual concerns. These meetings can also be a time to communicate successes and ideas. The administrators and counselors can also meet with the teaching teams regularly. Another option is for the leader from each teaching team to meet regularly with the administrators and counselors.

Yet those meetings are not enough to build full awareness. The administrator who continually interacts with colleagues and with students with sincere conversations about problems, victories, progress, concerns, and day-to-day and moment-to-moment matters is increasingly aware of circumstances at school, is more able to stop a small problem from becoming a larger problem, is more likely to be at or near the right place at the right time to help resolve an emerging problem, and is constantly building a school-wide network of partnerships, alliances, bonds, and commitments. Sincere, continuous interaction builds awareness and creates opportunities for helpful responses at the moment of interaction and as later follow-up. An example follows.

The principal of a middle school is walking through the school hallways during first period class. He has visited each class on a 6th grade team this morning. As he returns to the office in response to a text message from a secretary, he sees one of the school's two guidance counselors. Just saying hello is not enough. The principal begins a quick but helpful conversation, which is how he usually interacts with colleagues and, whenever possible, with students.

"Thanks very much for the extra time you spent with that family yesterday afternoon. Those are complicated issues, but your ideas gave them a lot of direction. Let me know whenever something with that student or her family comes up again. There will probably need to be a lot of follow-up. I saw the student at breakfast today. I was glad she could be at school today with all that family told us yesterday. Anything you are working on today that I could help with?"

The counselor knew that the offer of help was genuine because all prior offers had always been followed with action. "Yes, please. I'll meet during 6th period with the 7th grade Explorers team. The teachers have a concern about one group of students who just started bullying some other students. This same team has a great idea for a creative way to connect math and science classes and instruction. If you can join us for that meeting it would be great."

The principal was glad to be involved. "I'll be there. Let's get right on the bullying problem immediately. We need names, facts, accusations, evidence. Let's stop that now. In fact, I'll go see the team leader now. The math and science plan sounds interesting. I'll see everyone at that meeting. I'll need to eat a quick lunch after 5th period, but I'll be there."

Contrast that with the principal politely greeting the counselor with "Hello," and then walking to his destination. What the principal did was efficient, personal, and productive. He interacted. He built upon his working relationship with the counselor. He was face-to-face with the counselor anyway, but he made the most of the encounter. He made this interaction part of his leadership and management work. He began solving the bullying problem now.

He is alerted to a bullying problem and to an instructional opportunity in a school building and with an age group of students where building relationships is an essential ingredient of success. The principal showed by example how to do that. The counselor is supported and encouraged. The 7th grade teaching team will be helped, supported, listened to, and guided. Students will benefit as bullying is stopped and as creative instruction is developed.

Some of the circumstances, situations, and issues that middle school counselors deal with, investigate, and seek to resolve can be heartbreaking, can drain the last unit of energy from the body, and can exhaust the soul. The aware and responsive middle school administrator will notice when such ordeals occur and will provide the encouragement, support, and opportunities for renewal that the most capable school counselor can need after the most complex of interactions. Something as simple as walking outside around the building with the counselors could be ample support to acknowledge their good work and to help them endure.

The school must be cleaned and maintained daily. Meals must be prepared and served daily. Phones must be answered continually. People coming to the office throughout each day must be greeted and assisted. The office records and school accounting must be maintained.

The people who do these jobs are part of the staff that helps enable a middle school to thrive, or are part of the staff that just help a middle school get by, or are part of the staff that lets a middle school underperform. All of these people can be guided by, encouraged by, acknowledged by, listened to, and inspired by a middle school principal who is aware, involved, responsive, and genuine.

During daily cafeteria duty at breakfast and/or lunch, school administrators can interact with the cafeteria staff and with all other staff members who come to the cafeteria. There is no reason to dread cafeteria duty when it is seen as an efficient way to have personal, face-to-face interaction with almost every person who is at school daily.

One difference between a middle school custodian who works just enough to not get fired and a middle school custodian who excels with a work ethic that ensures that the school will always look immaculate and will always be maintained correctly can be a middle school administrator who convinces that custodian of the direct link between a school building that glows and students, faculty, and staff who glow. Good work can be appreciated and should be appreciated. We get more of what we reward.

Many school administrators may contend that the office secretaries really run the school. The essence of that statement reflects the reality that the secretaries interact with so many people continually throughout the day that they seem to have their hand on the pulse of the school. The impression made by these secretaries on people at school or on people who visit school can be a major factor in how some people perceive the school.

As with all staff members and teachers, the principal must insist that everyone does his or her job fully and correctly. That is a condition of those people being employed, but the astute middle school administrator goes beyond getting mere job description compliance from school staff members. The principal shows these key people how much they can contribute to school through what they do and how they do it. This principal builds a middle school community by making everyone at school realize their importance to the community. An example follows.

The cafeteria staff of a middle school is not simply cooking food. This cafeteria staff is not only preparing meals for students. This cafeteria staff is serving food to middle school students who notice everything that other people do. The cafeteria staff can exemplify manners and require that students are mannerly with them. The cafeteria staff can ask students for menu ideas and build relationships with students by preparing some of those suggestions for menu items in the near future.

The cafeteria staff can work with teaching teams to have meals that match with academic content. When 6th graders are studying European geography, the cafeteria can have some European items on the menu along with European pictures on the walls of the cafeteria. A middle school administrator who fosters such teamwork, partnerships, and interaction is a leader who seeks to make every moment a time of learning, of valuable experience, and of helping middle school students navigate the middle school maze throughout the school day no matter what part of the building they are in or what activity they are experiencing.

The purpose of a school is to cause learning. Most learning at school occurs in the classrooms or because of what happens in classrooms. Additional learning can occur throughout each day and throughout the school building. A perfectly clean building, a building where preventive maintenance keeps everything in proper working order, a building where precautions for safety are taken, a building where student-created signs artistically decorate the walls with messages of encouragement, a building where guests are sincerely welcomed immediately upon arrival is a building where learning is enhanced because the total environment supports learning.

This environment also creates additional learning as the students notice the priorities and the practices of this school are reflected in what everyone who works here does. The school administrators are in key positions to help create and to help maintain the total learning atmosphere, environment, and standards throughout the entire school.

Books can be written about how educators should work with parents and guardians of students. That substantial topic merits some attention here, yet is the detailed subject of other extended considerations. What is a middle school capable of doing with and for the parents or guardians of middle school students that provides the insight, guidance, encouragement, direction, and partnership that the middle school years create a unique need for?

Middle school educators have known hundreds, thousands of middle school students. Each parent and each guardian knows only one or a few family members who are or have been middle school students. No adult knows a middle school student better than the parents or guardians of the student. The combined insights, wisdom, concerns, and successes of the teachers based on experiences through the classroom years plus those of families through the childhood and early adolescent years at home can merge to form the possibility of unlimited understanding of each student, which helps identify precise educational programming for each student.

Some parents and guardians are very comfortable coming to school. Other parents and guardians may avoid any time at school. From e-mail to phone calls to home visits, contact can be made. The middle school principal or assistant principal who, by example, relentlessly reaches out to families of students can increase family involvement in, participation with, and support for the middle school.

If homework information, school news, cafeteria procedures, bus schedules, school directory, daily school announcements, grading policies, discipline system, reward system, school schedule, school calendars, and answers to frequently asked questions are posted on the school's Web site, the communication process with families is strengthened. If all of that information is also in print to distribute to each family and to have copies in the office to offer to everyone who enters the office, the communication process is further strengthened.

When every teaching team adds more information daily about homework, news, events, and tests, the communication expands further. Parents and guardians need to know all about school. So tell them often and thoroughly. Set as a goal that no parent or guardian who makes an effort to be informed would ever say "I did not know that" about any important aspect of the middle school.

A middle school principal decides to call three families per day just to establish a dialogue. She also has the assistant principal and both counselors call three other families per day. In two or three months, each family associated with the school was contacted personally. This example is followed by each teaching team making one or two phone calls to families per day. If e-mail works better, that is an option, but it should not be a weakened substitute just to claim that some effort was made to send information.

The effective middle school administrator practices the leadership and management guideline of "be there" in the classroom, in the hallways, in the cafeteria, in the bus loading area, in the school, virtually everywhere at all times. Parents and guardians can increasingly have a "be there" awareness of school if the communication between school and families is constant, thorough, sincere, cordial whenever possible, and diplomatically blunt whenever necessary.

Go one step beyond communication and invite parents and guardians to be at school when their schedule permits or when their schedule has to be adjusted to show the priority that school is. When parents and guardians can actually be there at school and when they know their presence is welcomed, appreciated, sought, and productive, the middle school learning environment is supported and the middle school maze now has some additional guides who can more directly help middle school students, one at a time, along the journey.

The tone of this book is intentionally designed to be hopeful, optimistic, and encouraging. Why? Because the ideal is for a middle school to be a hopeful, optimistic, encouraging place. Reality demands this caution—some parents and guardians are very difficult to deal with. For a variety of reasons or motivations, some parents and guardians resent educators, dislike school, are belligerent, are vulgar, seek to be dramatic to perform for their ego rather than seek to cooperate for their child's human growth and development.

In dealing with such unreasonable people, never descend to the level of belligerent, vulgar, confrontational, unreasonable, or unprofessional. "I understand that you think the situation was unfair, yet the major issue is your child's success at school. She decided to not do the homework. She decided to not answer any questions on the test. This is not good for her, for you, or for her teacher. The issue is your child's success at school. Let's avoid name-calling and concentrate on what needs to be done to make sure your daughter improves and succeeds."

If that statement is greeted with more belligerence and vulgarity, repeat the statement calmly and verbatim. For interactions such as these, have another administrator or a counselor in the meeting with you. If no progress is made, let the parent or guardian know that it is time to agree to disagree and it is time to involve the next level in the chain of command. Sincerely thank the person for coming, wish them a good day, and confirm that you will continue working for their child's success at school.

On the more encouraging side, a middle school administrator often can get much volunteer time and effort from a parent organization. This group can help with everything from making copies for teachers to decorating the cafeteria on special occasions, from organizing efficient communication networks among all parents to helping set up family activities at school on Open House night. By the time students are in middle school, some students and their families are well acquainted from having shared the elementary school years together. Middle school administrators can tap into this ready-made network of friendships, talents, interests, and volunteering.

In dealing with middle school students, what are the priorities for a middle school administrator? The survey results emphasized getting to know the students, building relationships with students, fostering an academic program designed for middle school students, remembering what is age-effective with middle school students, remembering the unique attributes of middle school students who are navigating their a-maze-ing years, and continuing being a middle school educator even though you are a middle school administrator rather than a middle school teacher.

The building must be managed. The faculty, staff, and students must be led. Decisions must be made. Priorities must be established and abided by. Laws, regulations, and policies must be implemented and followed. Budget decisions must be made and obeyed. Directives from upper-level management must be followed. Emergencies must be addressed. In the midst of these realities, which can absorb a full day's time and energy, how does a middle school administrator continue to be an authentic middle school educator?

By doing the administrative duties of leadership and management with the mind of an administrator combined with the heart of a teacher. Leaving the classroom to become an administrator does not require leaving behind the heart and soul of an educator and transforming into a regulated, bureaucratic, mechanized executive who overlooks people in the pursuit of systems, programs, and procedures.

Every decision made, every conversation shared, every public address announcement made, every classroom visited, every student encountered, provide middle school administrators with continuing opportunities to lead and manage in ways that reflect, apply, and support the goals of a middle school. Lead and manage with the same student-centered devotion that teachers are expected to teach with. Add to that an equivalent devotion to the faculty and staff of a school so that with all interactions, the work of an administrator always builds, strengthens, and expands the potential goodness of the middle school environment.

It is necessary to say no. Good leaders and good managers know when and why to say no. Some behaviors by students are wrong and they must be told that. Their misbehavior gets a firm no. In many interactions with students the principal can express a vibrant yes, which communicates sincere interest in the student, concern for the student, encouragement to the student, and inspiration for the student. It can be as simple as telling a student during lunch how impressive his answer in U.S. history class was earlier in the day. Such interaction costs no money and requires no extra time; rather it requires taking the initiative to do the best work at all times. It would be sad to wonder what could have been done if only more initiative had been exercised.

Why not see yourself as the teacher of all teachers and the one person who can be the teacher of all students? "Because there is so much else to do. The meetings. The phone calls. The e-mails. The emergencies. The, you know, the stuff that only the administrators can do." That stuff never ends. That stuff can be cursed and then done just to get rid of it. Or that stuff can be done in ways and with an attitude that makes even the most routine stuff energized with the most certain devotion to creating the best possible middle school.

The "what" never ends and is part of a school administrator's job reality. How the "what" is done is purely up to the administrator. This is part of a school administrator's freedom and power to consistently lead, manage, teach by example, to continually, minute-by-minute, day-by-day, make the middle school the ideal it can be for all involved to benefit from, contribute to, and thrive in.

For many more details on school administration, the reader is encouraged to read two of my other books, *The Extreme Principle: What Matters Most, What Works Best* (Rowman & Littlefield, 2011) and *911: The School Administrator's Guide to Crisis Management* (Rowman & Littlefield, 1996).

In dealing with middle school students, most of whom seek to please adults and most of whom watch closely to see how adults treat students, this concept can work wonders: Reward whenever possible, discipline whenever necessary.

Middle school students can be very quick to conclude, "That's not fair." These students are not law-school-educated experts in justice. "That's not fair" could mean "That's too much work" or "That's too hard" or "That means I can't go to the game today." Astute middle school administrators can be one step ahead of the "that's not fair" complaint, rationalization, or excuse.

"You disobeyed the clear and reasonable instructions of the teacher. You know the classroom rules. I have a copy of the page of rules, which you signed to show you are informed of the rules. The teacher told you twice to stop talking. Then she moved you to another desk. What's not fair is that your selfish misbehavior disrupted the work the teacher is required to do. It's interesting, the same teacher sent me eight names of students who behaved perfectly in the class. I will go to the class soon to give those eight students a free pass to a school sports event and a coupon for free pizza at the sporting event. You have seen me do the same thing in your math class. So, this is very fair. Students who behave get rewarded. Students who misbehave get penalized. If you prefer rewards to penalties, then behave."

The student had one question to ask. "What kind of pizza do they get at the game?"

That is not the question the school principal expected, but it does reveal what got the attention of that 7th grader. "Oh, they have choices—cheese or pepperoni or sausage." The student pretended to be in pain as he said, "Pepperoni? I love pepperoni pizza. I've got to get rewarded. What can I do?"

"Great question. I'll e-mail your teachers and tell them that after you finish the penalty today they can expect perfect behavior from you. If we go one week and I hear no bad news, plus I hear some good reports about you, I'll give you a pizza coupon."

The student smiled broadly. "Yes, sir. You can count on me." "Reward whenever possible" just combined with "punish whenever necessary" to create a moment when the principal was correcting a student as he also taught the student in an age-effective, middle-school-maze-navigating way. The days of a middle school administrator are filled with such moments that can create symbiotic results or that could be impersonal, bureaucratic, and "You misbehaved. You'll be in the in-school suspension room the rest of the day. Be sure there are no more problems."

There are times when "punish whenever necessary" must be harsh, severe, and rigid. Be decisive, firm, and serious in such situations. At other times, when creative flexibility offers a combined discipline action and lesson learned that could help avoid future discipline actions, be creative and flexible while still punishing according to policies. When discipline can include teaching, the administrator is law enforcer and educator, with a bit more of the educator coming through by design.

In the next chapter, much more detail will be presented and explored about providing school counseling services to students. The school counselor's duties and opportunities will be considered more completely than in this chapter, which centered, in terms of school counselors, on the interaction of middle school administrators and middle school counselors. The extremes of emotions, friends becoming enemies, harmful trends, gossip, "Who am I?" discoveries, and other middle school realities will be presented with emphasis on what middle school counselors can do and how they can best do that.

Chapter Five

Middle School Counselors

Counselor: Your English teacher gave me a copy of the paper you wrote for class yesterday. The assignment, as I understand it, was to think about the day you graduate from high school and everything you hope to accomplish between now and then. She said this is a project that 8th graders do each year right before you meet with some high school counselors to start making decisions about the classes you will take in 9th grade. Do you know why your English teacher gave me a copy of the paper you wrote?

8th Grader: Uh, not really. I didn't think anyone would read it except, I guess, the teacher and, you know, I didn't think she'd get all excited about what I wrote. I just had to write something to turn in, it wasn't any big deal.

Counselor: Your teacher was concerned. She read every word of your paper, twice. So did I. You wrote that on the day you graduate from high school you would like to see some empty chairs. It sounds like there are some students you would prefer are not there. That makes me think that you and some other 8th graders are not getting along. And unless they need to honor or remember someone respectfully, the high schools don't set up chairs at graduation for people who are not there unless something serious happened and the person cannot be there. So, let's figure out what you meant by saying you hope there are some empty chairs at your high school graduation.

8th Grader: It's nothing, really, you know, I mean, it's nothing. I didn't mean much. I guess there are some people I just don't like and I wish they would go away, that's all. I didn't mean anything bad. It's just, well, it's those girls who think they are better than everyone else. They wear new clothes. They have new cell phones. They never get in trouble even if they do something wrong. They get involved in everything. They think they're better than everyone else. They never speak to you. I just get tired of being around them.

Counselor: Tell me, have these other girls ever said anything or done anything to you? Have they made comments that bothered you? Or have they done something, like start a rumor about you or threaten you?

8th Grader: Not really, well, not much. Last week one of them took my seat in the cafeteria. I got up to take my tray back and when I went back to the table one of them had taken my seat. I never sit near them but that day there was no place else. She wouldn't get up. I just walked away and it was time to leave soon. But I thought that was unfair.

Counselor: Did something else happen after that?

8th Grader: Sort of. There was this note the next day in my locker. It said I needed to sit somewhere else at lunch and it said I needed to eat less at lunch. I know it was from them. I just wish they would leave me alone. They have their friends and I have my friends.

Counselor: I'll need to know who is involved in this. Write down their names and put the person who is bothering you most at the top of the list. Now, tell me if there is anything you have said to them or done to them. I'll get their side of the story from them, but you need to tell me about things like that. Have you said or done anything to them?

8th Grader: Uh, no. I don't think so.

Counselor: Is that the truth?

8th Grader: Uh. Well, like, I mean, you know once or twice I said something back at them, but I don't start it. They start it. I get really mad when they tease my best friend. She works really hard at school and school is tough for her, but she makes good grades and stuff. They tease her because she makes better grades than they do. They say she cheats. So, I take up for my friend. And I think I know who put that note in my locker, so I hid her English book in the classroom. She'll never find it. I guess I need to help her find it or something like that. Maybe I'll just tell the teacher where it is and act like I found it.

Counselor: That would not be honest, would it? You and I will talk to the teacher. She is on planning period now, so this is a good time. Be sure you don't say or do anything else to these other girls. I'll meet with them today and get their side of the story. I'll let the principal know about this. Maybe today or it might be tomorrow we'll get you and the other students together or maybe just one or two of them so we can resolve this. Depending on what I find out, we'll know what actions need to be taken. Remember, don't say or do anything else. Don't tell people why I brought you to the office. Don't send text messages or e-mail or anything like that about all of this. One more question. Were you and any of these other girls ever friends, maybe last year or earlier this year or back in elementary school?

8th Grader: They aren't my friends.

Counselor: I realize that, but how about in the past? Were you friends with any of them before?

8th Grader: Sort of. Well, yes. Last year I was friends with Janice, but then she changed. When she came back to school this year she was always with that other group. I asked her if we were still friends and, you know, she just pretty much ignored me. Why are people like that? I thought we were friends. Somebody told me that Janice's mom got remarried last summer and her stepfather is rich. So Janice thinks she's cool and better than her old friends so she got in with that other group. This is all so stupid.

Counselor: Let's get it worked out. It's on your mind and maybe other people are concerned about it, too. Let's go see your English teacher and take care of that book. Is it possible that the book belongs to Janice?

8th Grader: Maybe. Well, yeah. But I didn't steal it or anything. I just needed to mess with her.

Counselor: Would you like for someone to hide your books? Would you like for someone to mess with you like that?

8th Grader: I guess not. But all of this isn't fair. I didn't start it.

Counselor: Well, let's go take care of that book so no matter who started this we can all help stop it.

The discussion between the middle school counselor and the 8th grade student took a few minutes. The follow-up investigation, mediation, meetings, communication, plan of action to implement and monitor would require many hours spread out over several days. While working on this one situation, the same middle school counselor has multiple duties that overlap, multiple requests for help that cannot be scheduled in a perfectly orderly way, and many responsibilities in the official job description and in the unofficial, but very real, minute-to-minute work that is within the continual process of guiding hundreds of eleven- to fourteen-year-old students through the middle school maze.

The counselor walked to class with the 8th grader. Why not just give the student a note to take with her to class? The counselor had learned through the years that after a complex conference with a student, three minutes of time walking with the student back to class was a wise investment.

These three minutes assured that the student did, in fact, get back to class rather than wander around. These three minutes also assured that there would be no incident on the way back to class or upon returning to class. Why take the chance that this student could encounter one of the girls she is having problems with as she returns to class? The years of doing outstanding work as a middle school counselor had revealed what works and what does not work. On the way back to the office, an 8th grade teacher spoke to the counselor in the hall.

Teacher: Do you have a moment, please? I really need to ask you a question.

Counselor: Sure. Would you rather talk here or go in my office?

Teacher: Let's go in your office. That will be better. (Now in the office.) Yes, this is better. Well, I'm not sure where to start and I'm not sure you are the right person, but you can tell me. This is my first year of teaching, you know that. I get here really early every day and I stay late. Then I go home and work more. I work all weekend on school stuff. It's the only way to keep up. Well, it's too much. It's just too much.

And so many of the students just don't care. I prepare great lessons for my classes. I grade papers immediately so they get papers back in a day or two. I keep in touch with their families to report any good news and to ask for help with misbehavior or with academic problems. Some families are supportive. Other families just seem to think it's our job to fix all of that. So, I'm just really not sure what to do next. Is it like this for every teacher? Is it always going to be like this?

Counselor: Those are really important questions. We can figure out some answers and some ideas. There are several teachers who you can get great advice from. The principal certainly needs to hear from you about this. Have you talked to anyone else yet?

Teacher: I talked to another new teacher. She said the same thing. It's more work than she ever expected and it was hurting her life outside of school. She's been married a year and all of this time she spends on school is taking time away from her marriage. She made a lot of changes. She gives less homework and she gives fewer tests. She's still, you know, doing a good job.

They have enough homework and enough tests, but not so many as they once did, and she decided to do no schoolwork on weekends. From Friday afternoon through coming back to school on Monday, she is all about her husband and their marriage. She says things are much better. It bothers her a little that she could be doing more for her students, but she says that she signed a contract to teach and she committed herself to vows of marriage. She says the contract is for a year. The marriage is for life.

Counselor: Have you considered any of the changes the other teacher made as possibilities for yourself?

Teacher: Not really. I mean, like, I expect a lot of myself. I just don't know if this job is even possible to do. The students don't work very hard. They get in trouble. Some of them try and do behave, but this just isn't what I thought it would be. I got my master's degree right after college. I know this stuff. My knowledge of math is really good. I thought I had been around students enough to be ready, but this sure is not what I anticipated. I'm determined to keep making the effort. I'm just not sure that enough effort is humanly possible to deal with all of this. What should I do?

Counselor: Here's my idea. I'd like to ask the teacher who is your team leader to meet with you, the principal, and me. Let's all think this through. There are ideas we can share with you and others we can create together. Your teaching team may be able to help with certain students. The principal is an expert on career stuff like this. He has worked with so many new and experienced teachers that he is a perfect resource; plus, topics like this are in his job description more than in anyone else's, but a lot of us can help. I'll set up a meeting for tomorrow either during your planning period or after school. Will that work?

Teacher: Sure. Thanks a lot. I hope this is not taking your time away from other stuff you need to do.

Counselor: Don't give that a thought. You deserve my time and I'm eager to help. Let's team up to make things better for you and for your work with the students. I'll let you know as soon as I have that meeting set up.

The counselor does not see herself as a career guide for teachers, but she can help organize this meeting and then defer to the principal, who has personnel authority. The principal also evaluates teachers, counselors, and staff. The counselor was not going to dismiss the teacher, but the counselor knows that issues like this are more within the duty of and the responsibility of the principal. She has worked with this principal for eight years. She knows he would expect her to be caring and helpful in situations like this, yet she also knows that he would expect to be informed quickly and to be involved fully.

The pace did not slow down on this day. The pace for a conscientious middle school counselor rarely, maybe never, slows down.

A 7th grade student was with the middle school's assistant principal as they both walked toward the school counselor's office. There were two counselors at this school so each counselor worked with half of the students in each grade. That gave each counselor about 350 students to work with, far too many to completely provide services to everyone. The school administration repeatedly asked the school district to provide a third counselor so each grade level could have a counselor. The request was rejected annually.

The principal, assistant principal, and counselors dreamed of and lobbied for staffing allocations that would provide three counselors. The plan was for one counselor to work with the 6th graders, and to keep working with those students as they became 7th graders, then as they became 8th graders. Strong relationships could be established and developed to enhance the services provided. The school district said that the budget constraints were too severe. The leaders of this middle school thought that school district officials needed to spend a week in a middle school to realize what reality is.

Still, the counselors at this middle school were determined to help students in every way their jobs permitted and their time demands allowed. Time—there was never enough. The assistant principal politely asked the counselor, "I know it's another busy day, but we were hoping you had a few minutes to see us. There's a situation you can help with. Will that work?"

The answer is yes. The answer has to be yes. The assistant principal and the counselors have worked together for years. When they ask each other for help it is understood that help is needed now.

The assistant principal continued as everyone settled into the office. "I had a discipline referral today about Katy and it just seemed so unusual because it had never happened before. Not in 6th grade and not this year in 7th grade. She had really disrupted class with loud and threatening comments to another student. There's more to it than that. Katy, tell Ms. Bellton what you told me. I know it's a difficult subject, but let's all work together."

Katy was silent for a moment. She then got a few words out. "It's, it's, it's my parents. They are getting…" At that point Katy was in tears. The assistant principal handed Katy a tissue and then told the counselor that Katy's parents were getting divorced. The middle school years have enough complexities without adding a family matter as serious as divorce.

The assistant principal decided that Katy and Ms. Bellton could work best on this matter if he left them to talk in confidence. He told Katy he would keep in close touch with her by talking at lunch and stopping by some of her classes occasionally. He asked Ms. Bellton to keep him informed of anything he could do. He told Katy he would let her teacher know that she was with the counselor. He also said that the conference with him, the time with the counselor, and an act of school service would resolve the discipline referral. School service gave students a chance to do something beneficial for the school to make up for something that had been hurtful to the school.

Ms. Bellton was always kind, caring, thoughtful, and compassionate. In circumstances such as these she doubled those expressions. Katy is an excellent student who always makes the Honor Roll, who is on the school's academic team, and who plays on the school's volleyball team. Now Katy was distraught because what mattered most to her was changing in a way she never expected and in a way that she had no idea how to cope with. Ms. Bellton had dealt with students of divorce many times, but she knew that those other times did not change anything about the anguish that Katy was experiencing.

Ms. Bellton knew that her job did not include evaluation of or intervention in the family matters that impacted Katy. Her job was to support Katy so the Honor Roll, academic team, volleyball team student she was could continue to grow. Ms. Bellton hoped that while Katy's home life moved through a time of uncertainty and turmoil, that school could be a place of continued achievements, certainty, and peace. It would be difficult for Katy to maintain her school success as she endured complete change in her family structure, but Ms. Bellton was dedicated to providing all possible support. As Ms. Bellton continued talking with Katy, the student was not the only person in tears. Being a middle school counselor can have its times of heartbreak.

Is a school counselor job virtually identical at the elementary school, middle school, and high school levels, or is there uniqueness in each job? For the specific purposes of this book the question becomes: Are there unique characteristics of the middle school counselor's work due to the unique attributes and realities of middle school in general and of middle school students in particular? The survey insights will help answer that specific middle school question.

The survey question that most directly relates to the work of a middle school counselor asked, "On the 'Human growth and development/Who am I' side, what experiences and opportunities should middle school include?" Responses follow.

- "As many varieties of activities as possible, both scholastic and intramural."

- "Antibullying curriculum. Suicide prevention. Programs for children of alcoholics and other programs to stop middle schoolers from drinking alcohol. Development of individual learning plans instead of a generic plan for everyone."
- "Students would benefit from more time to socialize with friends and teachers. Perhaps a longer lunch time?"
- "Opportunities for students to develop autonomy, to pursue self-exploration, to understand the expectations of society for norms and values."
- "Extracurricular activities such as clubs, sports, dances—anything to get students involved and trying new things. Encourage them to join others and feel ownership of their school."
- "Visits to work places—immersion in the arts and cultural activities to explore creativity and to express individuality."
- "Character education–based messages throughout the curriculum. Prejudice reduction and sensitivity-to-others activities."
- "They must have a social curriculum to teach character building and dealing with pressures they face as teenagers growing up physically and emotionally."
- "Community service projects and character education. Both are very important."
- "Many middle schoolers are not comfortable in their own skin yet, so expose them to various real-world experiences such as the arts, sports, clubs, and other activities to enhance the idea of lifelong learning."
- "Opportunities for students to have a voice in how the class is taught, a choice in assignments, the right to feel empowered."
- "More information about impulse control, expressing feelings and emotions in the proper way and place at school. Bullying information. Identifying people in the building who can help and where those people are."
- "More time to discuss issues. Require students to participate in activities during as well as before or after school. Help them realize they are not the only one experiencing things. Show them that middle school is not like the scripted television programs with thirteen-year-old characters portrayed by older actors."

Consider the situation presented at the start of this chapter with the survey comments. The situation realistically shows that problems, issues, concerns, difficulties, needs, complications, and problems will find their way to middle school counselors. Part of the middle school counselor's job is to respond to these circumstances as they arise.

The survey insights suggest that there is a power in "preacting." The optimistic aspect of this is that, for example, if more character education could result in less bullying, the middle school environment would be more wholesome, the middle school students would be less subject to verbal or other abuse, the number of bullying incidents would decrease, and more concentration on academic work could occur.

What is the difference between "All acts of bullying will be investigated and punished" and "All acts of kindness will be appreciated and rewarded"? It is extremely and unrealistically idealistic to think that zero acts or words in the bullying category would occur when seven hundred students aged eleven to fourteen gather daily. It is not idealistic to create an atmosphere where such actions and words are rare because everyone is taught to treat people the way they would like to be treated, because the adults exemplify the desired behaviors, and because the students who do what is right are acknowledged. Some students may need to be taught that bullying is wrong, is unacceptable, is not allowed, and is just not done here.

How can middle school counselors help lead the way to create this middle school atmosphere, environment, and reality where students, faculty, and staff work in a mutual commitment of concern, discipline, cooperation, fairness, and doing what is right?

The term "team spirit" usually applies to athletics. Participants on a sporting team are fully expected by their coaches, by each other, and by themselves to work hard, encourage one another, follow team rules, follow the sport's rules, and display the character that makes champions. Team spirit need not be owned exclusively by athletics.

A middle school can have an overall spirit that "We are in this together, we are a learning team, we are a team in progress, we are a team strengthened by individual effort and mutual commitments." Sounds good, but how does it happen? What can middle school counselors do to help make it happen? Isn't the overall school direction, organization, and way of doing things under the authority of the principal working with the assistant principal and their colleagues?

Good point. There is a management structure and a chain of command. Would a principal reject a middle school counselor's request for the counselor to visit classes and teach an anti-bullying curriculum? More information is required. Teachers need to be involved in that decision because it impacts their instructional time. The principal needs to consider the few concerns about having a counselor out of the office and the many possible gains of this direct instruction.

If all arrangements could be made and if everyone impacted did agree, then a middle school counselor could lead the way to implement an anti-bullying program. The following example shows one approach.

"We need to talk. You and I, right now, right here, we need to talk. We need to hear each other, listen to each other, respect each other, and appreciate each other.

"We need to TALK, which stands for Together A Lot of Kindness. There are twenty-seven students, one 6th grade teacher, and one counselor in this room right now. Each of us can say something kind to someone every day. Our goal is to stop bullying at this school, but that is only half of the work we need to do. The other half of our work is to start being more friendly, more kind, more thoughtful. Bullying is bad. Kindness is good. It's that simple.

"We need some examples. If a student is in the hallway and drops the three books she is carrying, the wrong thing to do is to kick the books around or to tease her about dropping them. The friendly and kind action is to help her pick up the books. It's so easy to do what is right. Now, let's see what examples you can think of for acts of kindness at school." Four hands went up quickly.

Student 1: I know. At lunch we can take our tray back and clean up any mess at our table.

Student 2: Maybe we can volunteer for the next campus cleanup project.

Student 3: We can help substitute teachers. They are always kind of confused so we can do things for them.

Student 4: We can show a new student around the school. It's not easy coming to a school where you don't have any friends, so we can be friends to new students.

That idea sparked a thought from one more student who said, "We could be friends to old students. We have known each other, some of us, since kindergarten. But we have our group of friends. We could talk to people we never talk to."

The counselor continued the presentation to and interaction with this group of 6th graders. During this week she would make nine more presentations to other 6th grade classes. Each presentation would take about thirty minutes. She would visit the classes once per week for three weeks to follow up in hopes of hearing good news about people being kind and friendly. She would also measure the number of bullying incidents in the 6th grade during this month. Her hope was to see less bullying than the prior month and to hear of many acts of kindness.

After the 6th grade TALK program completed its first month and was evaluated, the program would be improved as needed and then implemented with 7th graders one month, followed by 8th graders the next month. The counselor's hope was that the school would have a vibrant celebration at the end of the semester to reward academic achievement and to reward acts of kindness. She thought that athletes always get cheers and rewards and awards, but such attention sends a message that sports are the top priority. What a school celebrates and rewards shows the school's priorities.

In addition to encouraging kindness, the TALK program enables the counselor to interact with every 6th grader once a week for a month. These initial interactions can be a foundation for building the types of relationships that are so meaningful to middle school students and that are a key emphasis in the survey responses considered thus far.

There is also a time management factor with the TALK program. A bullying incident is harmful and hurtful to the people involved. Such incidents are disruptive to the school overall. A school counselor may need to spend several hours to help investigate and resolve a bullying incident. The TALK program invests time in a preactive way that can reduce bullying. The hours invested in TALK can reduce the hours spent on a bullying investigation while increasing the favorable, friendly, kind acts in the school.

Preventing an act of bullying means a student does not have to experience the anguish, the confusion, the emotional pain of wicked comments or evil actions. Preventing such harm is one way of promoting human growth and development. Preventing students from becoming bullies or from becoming victims of bullies is clearly beneficial to everyone in the school. Counselors can help lead the way in an effort like TALK and in similar efforts that address other school problems or opportunities.

Middle schools are fertile ground for potentially unlimited impact by guidance counselors. Why? Because middle school students need frequent guidance through the maze that is the middle school years. Whether spoken or unspoken, middle school students are asking the question, "Who am I?" The answers are not necessarily permanent because the years between ages eleven and fourteen are so dynamic.

"I'm not the child I was in elementary school, so who am I now?"

"I need my parents to get stuff for me, but I need them to let me have some freedom and independence. So, who am I?"

"My best friend for years is not my best friend any more. Stuff like that happens, I guess. It's strange. Who is my best friend now? Do I have a best friend now? If my friends change, what's that mean? Who are my real friends? Who am I?"

"What makes my voice sound different? It's not a little child voice or a grown-up voice. It's in between. Who do I sound like now?"

"I hate math. It used to be such a cool class last year. Now it is so dumb. I hate math. I used to do great in math. How did I get to be dumb in math? What changed, me or math?"

"Everyone else is getting taller. I'm not. That's not fair. What's wrong with me? Will I ever grow?"

"Eighth grade is hard. Sixth and seventh grade were so easy. All I hear now is that we have to get ready for high school. My grades are down. Does that mean I'm not going to be ready for high school?"

"I didn't mean to say it. That teacher just doesn't like me. I didn't mean to say she was a bad teacher. She never calls on me. She never gives me an A on anything. I know some students who cheat and she never finds out. So I make a low grade, but I'm honest. They make a high grade and cheat. How is that fair?"

"She started it. She and I liked each other. Then she liked another guy. She never said nothing to me. She just ignored me. So I started some rumors about her. She deserved it. What was I supposed to do?"

From the time a five-year-old is in kindergarten to the time an eighteen-year-old graduates from high school, there is no three-year time period that is more turbulently fascinating than the middle school years. The educator who becomes a guidance counselor and who chooses to work in a middle school is working in a setting that poses unprecedented and unsurpassed challenges to students and opportunities for students. There simply are no limits to what each day can bring or to what could be achieved each day in a middle school where students are so clearly an a-maze-ing work in progress.

Middle school counselors sometimes hear this question from parents and guardians: "What happened to my child? She was so calm, steady, sensible, responsible, and trustworthy. Now she's calm one day and agitated the next day. She is reasonable one day and makes no sense the next day. We can trust her one day and then we become very suspicious the next day when she violates our trust. What happened to her? Will she ever be her old self again?"

Part of the answer is, "Your child is living in the extremes of middle school. These are years of drama, wonder, fear, curiosity, discovery, confusion, direction, misdirection, trials, errors, and successes, and much of that is done in extremes."

"The brains are still forming. Thinking skills are still developing. School is more challenging and that requires adjustments. Significant, once-in-a-lifetime physical changes are occurring and that can bring questions, fear, excitement, and comparisons. Childhood is not over, but it's not the same as during the elementary school years. The teenage years begin, but they are not what they will be like in the high school years. One reaction to all of this by some middle school students is to push to the extreme. School is great then school is awful. Friends are perfect then friends are stupid, then friends are perfect again. The middle school years are punctuated with extremes."

A guidance counselor sees, feels, hears, works with, and analyzes these extremes daily. The counselor provides wisdom and moderation for students who bounce between extremes. Where emotions run too high, the counselor brings a mature stability and shows the student a path to moderating emotions into a managed response rather than an outburst, an emotional explosion, or a moment of being stuck in a corner of the middle school maze. An example follows: Two middle school 8th grade students had the following exchange in the school cafeteria during lunch.

Bradley: Hey, I heard what you were saying. It's not true, Tommy, none of it.

Tommy: Yeah, right, Bradley. You know it's true. You like her, but she doesn't like you. She likes some 9th grader at the high school. Why would she like an 8th grader when some 9th grader likes her?

Bradley: Tommy, you need to shut up. At least I like a girl and I get out and do stuff with people. All you ever do is play video games in your basement.

Tommy: Bradley, you are so stupid. I have tons of friends come over to play those games. We have a great time. We do stuff. If you weren't so difficult to get along with, maybe I'd ask you to come play video games. Never.

Bradley: Tommy, I'd never come to your house. I have a better house. And look, there's the girl I like. She just looked at me. So I think she likes me. She doesn't care about any 9th grader. And she sure doesn't care about you.

Tommy: Bradley, you're dreaming. I'll go ask her if she likes you. Be right back.

Another student entered the developing confrontation. "Bradley, you better go ask her yourself. Tommy won't tell you the truth. He's just going to say that she doesn't like you no matter what she really says."

Bradley jumped up. He went toward the table where Tommy had gone. This was getting tense. Tommy turned around and said loudly, "Bradley, you lose. She doesn't like you."

That led to a push as Bradley used his hand to do his talking. Tommy pushed back as the assistant principal stepped in to separate them. A quick call to the office had a school counselor on the way to sort through this. The assistant principal would take discipline action. The counselor would help the students realize how they let this situation escalate and teach them how they could have handled this matter better.

As the counselor spent time with Bradley and Tommy she could benefit from work done earlier in the school year. During the first and second weeks of school this counselor met with each first period 8th grade class. The other counselor met with 7th grade classes on the same schedule. The assistant principal and the principal divided the 6th grade classes so they could spend extra time with the new students.

Part of what was discussed in those meetings was the technique of "Walk away and tell an adult." This was a method designed to de-escalate situations. The students were shown a short video of three middle school students who got into a loud verbal confrontation. Two alternative endings were shown. In one ending, the three students shout, get angry, push, shove, and get in trouble. In the other ending, two of the students walk away while the third student yells, but is ignored. The two students who walked away went separate directions, each found a teacher, and both teachers called a counselor to help.

The counselor made Bradley and Tommy watch the video. She made them write their version of the cafeteria situation. She made them each explain what could have been done better without blaming the other person or saying only what the other person should have done better.

The counselor listened closely to Bradley and Tommy. She required them to listen closely to each other with no interruptions. As the students were led by the counselor through the entire mediation process, they went from the cafeteria extreme of anger, jealousy, and embarrassment, all in front of an audience, to the sensible calm of mediation away from the crowd.

The assistant principal did take discipline action. The counselor did some follow-up the next day at lunch. She ate with the two students in the cafeteria. The students had to show themselves and the cafeteria crowd that yesterday's enemies could become today's friends, or at least could be friendly.

The discipline action was that Bradley and Tommy had to help clean the cafeteria for a week. This meant they had to work together to do something good for the school. By the end of the first day of their school service work they were talking to each other, listening to each other, and being friendly. It was all part of a middle school where teaching moments are found in every possible time and place. It was also part of a middle school where a lot of kindness was becoming the standard, the expectation, and the very intentionally learned behavior.

Do what you can with what you have. What do middle school counselors have? An endless number of opportunities each day to help guide middle school students through the maze into which an eleven-year-old enters and a fourteen-year-old exits. The number of wrong turns made, blockages encountered, and traps fallen into, walked around, or completely avoided throughout that maze can be impacted by the intentional, impactful, and interactive guidance provided by middle school counselors.

Teachers see their middle school students daily as students attend class. The opportunities for teachers to help guide students through the middle school maze are available every day and a conscientious, dedicated, determined teacher will maximize those daily opportunities.

A middle school guidance counselor works in an office, not in a classroom, so students are not automatically arriving daily to work with a counselor. Some students are sent to the counselor by a teacher or by an administrator. Some students are called to the office by a counselor. Some parents or guardians will come to school with a problem, issue, or question that requires a counselor's expertise and the student in that family may be included in the meeting or in part of the meeting.

Those encounters will enable a school counselor to interact with only a portion of the student body. School principals and assistant principals get to know the students who cause problems because those school administrators implement the discipline system. Principals and assistant principals must make an effort to meet, get to know, and interact with the many students who are not violating the school rules and who are, therefore, not sent to the office or written about in a discipline referral.

Counselors must spend time with students who are dealing with personal or interpersonal issues, problems, challenges, and situations. From suicide prevention to children of divorce, from drug use to bullying, from medication management to study skills, from the schedule of classes at school to the making of friends at school, from good academic habits in the classroom to good people skills in the hallways, from growing up socially to growing up physically, the school counselor will deal with matters related to these topics and more.

There are some middle school students whose circumstances will require that a school counselor spend time, perhaps repeatedly throughout a school year, with those students. For the many other students who are not as obviously in need of a counselor's intervention, how can a middle school counselor reach out to the students with less apparent needs and be supportive of or encouraging to students who are already making their way through the middle school maze with minimal difficulty or with seemingly no difficulty?

Be there. Be where the students are. The opportunities for interaction with students are presented daily and can be efficiently productive. Invest thirty minutes in the school cafeteria during lunch and there can be conversations with sixty students. Sit at a table with six students to ask them about their classes, their clubs, their sports, their ideas for school, their suggestions for what the cafeteria should serve, their ideas about the TALK program, reports on what acts of kindness they have been involved with recently, what school rule they think should change, and other topics that come up.

"But I don't have 30 minutes to be in the cafeteria for random conversations. I'm too busy."

That has much truth to it, yet that is exactly why investing those thirty minutes in the cafeteria is a great use of time. During a week of half-hour visits to the cafeteria a school counselor could see every student in the school and talk with a sizable number of the students. This cafeteria counseling builds new relationships, creates new communication, is itself an act of kindness, can help identify students whose comments in the cafeteria conversations may indicate a need for follow-up away from the crowd, and may provide some ideas or input to the counselor that otherwise would have been unspoken.

If a goal is to listen, listen more, keep listening, then the ears of the counselor must be where the students are talking. This does not replace listening closely during an office counseling meeting; rather, this complements that and supplements that. Some follow-up contact may just be a quick chat that can be done in the cafeteria, unless confidentiality is needed, and then the student could go with the counselor from the cafeteria to the office very simply and efficiently.

The author's confidence in cafeteria, hallway, sporting event, club meeting or similar situation counseling contact is based, in part, on thirteen years of supervising the before-school waiting area, the cafeteria, the hallways, and the bus loading area of a middle school. The opportunities for interaction were unlimited. From words of encouragement to words of correction, from "Great question you asked in class this morning" to "Your grades sure are up this semester," from "Tell me about that trip I heard you talking about" to "What classes did you sign up for when the high school counselor was here?" the results helped create a mutual awareness that, when properly nurtured, became a mutual commitment.

Is that idealistic? Yes, of course. To be an educator who prevails requires a large reservoir of idealism. Many of the realities faced by schools are harsh, difficult, frustrating, and worsening. To endure and to prevail amid such realities requires a clear understanding of reality and a relentless pursuit of the ideal.

A middle school counselor must bring an abundance of idealism, optimism, hope, and energy to school daily. These inner resources are needed because the realities at school will bring problems, pessimism, despair, and exhaustion. Confront the reality of the middle school maze with the confident certainty that there are paths to the victory line, the finish line, the exit.

One reality that must be confronted is that it is common for too few counselors to be at a middle school. Each counselor could be assigned to three hundred, four hundred, or more students. Now what?

The most serious situations must be given the top priority of time, attention, and effort. If 1 percent of the students assigned to a middle school counselor are involved in serious situations on a given day, much or most of the counselor's time on that day will be devoted to intervening and beginning to resolve those situations. Further time, attention, and effort could be needed in days that follow as the situation requires a continuation of guidance service. Now what?

Efforts could be made to ask the local school board to change the staffing formula so an additional counselor is provided. Budgets are limited so that option may face a blunt financial reality that says no. Keep asking. Help the authorities understand what is most needed.

What creative solutions exist or can be started to deal with the reality of too many students, too few counselors, and too little time? A time audit could help. Are there some paperwork tasks done now by counselors that a secretary at the school could do? Are there some noncounseling duties that, over the years or decades, have been assigned to middle school counselors that could be reassigned or that could be ended altogether? Is the job description for a middle school counselor dealing with today's reality or is that job description an evolved list of duties that, over the decades, have flowed to counselors and just never been updated?

The budget is limited. The job description may not change. Other school staff members may already have been assigned their capacity of tasks. Now what? Find efficiencies. For example, work with the teaching teams. Meet with one teaching team on Monday to hear from them about students who are of concern to them for various reasons that a counselor could help with. Meet weekly with the principal, assistant principal, team leaders, all counselors, and other colleagues such as a school social worker or school law enforcement officer to review confidentially the students everyone is working with in terms of counseling, discipline, at-risk behaviors, or other issues to be sure that each student is being helped while also making sure that two or three people are not duplicating efforts. If a counselor, assistant principal, and school social worker are each working directly with a student and the student's family, that can be streamlined to one person providing the services and the other people adding more support only as needed.

Of course, be there, but be there in various ways. When you visit a teacher's classroom to monitor a student you are working with, tell the teacher what was impressive about the lesson and the instruction. Teachers rarely are told that they are doing good work, even when they consistently do good or great work. It is rare for a student to compliment a teacher or to thank a teacher. Principals may occasionally send generic e-mails with content such as, "Thanks for the great work during the first week of this new school year," but that is superficial and ordinary. Build the emotional health of the school by sincerely and personally complimenting faculty, staff, and students who merit praise.

To be able to lead the way in creating a climate of genuine compliments, you have to be where the people who deserve the compliments are as much as possible. Sure, some guidance counselor work can be done only in the office, but school does not happen in offices so go where the people are and you'll be where the problems, possibilities, progress, opportunities, achievements, and awaiting compliments are.

A first-year middle school counselor who had been a 6th and 7th grade teacher for eleven years asked an experienced middle school counselor what had changed with middle school students over the three decades of his career. The expected answer was not heard; rather, the veteran counselor said the following:

"There is more that has not changed than there is that has changed. Middle school students have always had the growing-up transition issues to deal with. They have their extremes of emotions and interests. Today's friend is tomorrow's enemy. The student who never causes trouble can one day be in the middle of a big problem. Most of the students cooperate with the teachers most of the time.

"What has changed? Well, there are two areas. First, people who do not work in schools keep passing laws or policies or regulations that never work. Most of that stuff is trendy nonsense. Keeping up with those dumb changes takes time and rarely accomplishes anything good.

"Second, society is different. So many more students have family uncertainties. So many more students are on medications. Students spend so much time with video games, the Internet, cell phones, and electronic junk, they think the best use of their time is with some silly electronic gadget. They less and less do the real schoolwork of reading and thinking and writing. Their work ethic and their manners have declined. Why? The trash they see on television, in movies, or hear in popular music. They figure that rich entertainers or rich athletes are good examples to follow.

"There is something else. Electronic gadgets make problems get worse much faster. The old handwritten note that a student would write and pass to a friend could start a rumor. Now, some electronic text message that groups of students send to dozens of people starts a lot of rumors that cause lots of problems. That is getting worse and worse."

The first-year counselor was concerned and discouraged. "Is this a job that can still be done with any good results? You know, can I feel like I'm making a difference?"

The multi-decade experienced middle school counselor smiled and spoke with an almost reverent sincerity. "Yes, by directly, individually, person-to-person making a difference. We cannot do our job over the public address system. We cannot do our job through the school's morning announcements on television or with the school's Web site.

"When we do our job most effectively, we use the old-fashioned ways. We talk to people. We reach out to people. We encourage people. We guide people. We correct people. We support people. We counsel people. That is done person to person. Sure, you can make a difference. Your job puts you in a position where many differences can be made. So, take the initiative and make differences all day, every day."

"But there are so many students and so many problems. You said it gets worse every year or it gets more demanding or more serious. How do we keep up with everything?" The new counselor was determined but concerned about whether the job was too much for any one person.

The veteran had another idea to share based on years and years of experience. "One at a time. You make a difference with one student at a time. One student may need hours of your time. Another student may need minutes. Another student may just need a few friendly words day to day as you see each other in the hallway or in the cafeteria or at an after-school event. This is a job that needs you to make a difference and this job invites you or challenges you to take the initiative daily that will impact as many students as possible, as favorably as possible."

The experienced counselor paused and added one more thought. "Skip the conferences or meetings that would take you away from school on school days. Go to those, if you can find any that are worth attending, in the summer. On any day and on every day that students are at school, you need to be at school. To make the difference you seek to make you have to be with the people you seek to impact. Be at school, get out of your office often, and interact with students, teachers, and staff. That's how you make a difference over and over."

One source of an answer to the question "How have middle school students changed in recent years?" is found in academics. The middle school curriculum includes some classes at some schools that were exclusively taught in high schools a generation ago. When an 8th grader takes geometry and does well in that class, the later possibilities for very advanced math classes in high school expand.

Another answer could be seen in the extracurricular options at a middle school. The traditionally pure middle school concept of extracurricular activities stressed participation, ideally by each student, in a club or sport. Over time, perhaps because of illusions of professional greatness caused in part by continuous television coverage of athletic events, some people insist that middle school athletics should be the serious, intense, win-win-win training ground for future high school, college, and professional athletic superstars. As high school sports have become more intense, demanding, and competitive year-round endeavors, some people have worked to make middle school sports have a similar emphasis. Beware of that trend.

For middle school counselors, there is another trend in the category of what used to be in high school only but now in middle school. This list includes drug use including alcohol, pregnancy, violence, suicide, self-mutilation such inflicting cuts on oneself, skipping school, vicious bullying in person or via the Internet, social media misuse and/or addiction, obesity, and other serious concerns. The middle school maze has new complexities, places to get stuck, pitfalls, obstacles, decisions with long-term implications, and, tragically, some possibilities for real dead ends. The job of a middle school counselor requires blunt encounters with these realities that increasingly can harm, tempt, surround, intrigue, and agonizingly mislead middle school students.

Never has there been a more important time for middle school counselors to help create a school environment, atmosphere, process, support system, intervention method, and prevention plan of action through which middle school students can learn, mature, grow, achieve, and progress. The middle school maze will have some bumps along the path, but mountains or craters can be minimized, outsmarted, avoided, or prevented. Middle school counselors can be absolutely essential in leading the moment-to-moment work that helps maximize the goodness, the correctness, the learning, the discovery, and the wholesome wonder that can be the middle school experience for students.

This is a very demanding job through which differences that last a lifetime can be made. It is not a job for bureaucrats, office squatters, or eight-hour workdays. It is a job for people who promised themselves they would make a difference throughout a middle school, one student at a time, one moment at a time, until all students were reached as each moment was maximized.

Chapter Six

College Preparation Programs for Middle School Educators

First, abandon the theories. What matters most is doing what works best. Working in a middle school is a constant encounter with reality. Theories do not apply. Practical, realistic, certain, specific actions that work are needed.

"But the human growth and development concept I learned in college says that you are supposed to be an age group that seeks freedom, but needs structure. You are eleven or twelve years old, which puts you at a cognitive development stage of flux combined with new and dynamic social or emotional transitions that create potential moments of unintended disorder or atypical contrast with your usual conduct pattern. The theorists whose work I studied were certain that you could be trained to comply with the self-management chart and interaction conformity consensus techniques we worked on to respond politely when I give you a signal we practiced.

"Why is this class still talking even after I gave the signal we practiced and you signed a contract saying you would obey? Maybe I can ask my college professor about that." Abandon the theories. Deal with reality.

Second, we know what works, so relentlessly emphasize what works in the very real, very down-to-earth, very challenging, very exhausting, very frustrating, and very fascinating reality of teaching, counseling, and administration at a middle school. Action alone gets results. Experienced middle school educators have amassed an endless collection of instruction lessons that cause learning of productive projects, of useful homework assignments, of effective discipline systems and methods, of memorized phrases or sentences that are spoken to students in given situations, and of what to do or not do when encountering the bureaucracy of education.

For example, a 7th grade student used vulgar language in a classroom. The student's crude comment was directed at another student. When the teacher asked the student who spoke improperly "What were you thinking when you spoke that way knowing it violates the classroom rules and the school rules?" The student replies, "My brother is in high school. He told me to do that if anyone bothers me. My daddy said the same thing."

Notice, the teacher asked, "What were you thinking?" not "Why did you use vulgar language?" The "Why" question invites unproductive replies such as "I felt like it" or "Other people do that" or "That's what I heard on TV." The "What were you thinking" practiced question gets more revealing answers and is less likely to evoke excuses or rationalizations.

How can the teacher reply to the response about a brother or a father allegedly telling the 7th grader to use crude language? First, realize the answer may be dishonest. Second, do not respond in a way that creates a battle of loyalties. Third, do not take the bait and be critical of the student's family or that criticism will become the major issue rather than the verbal misbehavior of the student.

Consider this reply:

> At school, what we have to do can be different than what is done at home. We have bells and classes and a cafeteria at school. Home is not like that. The school has rules. Teachers have rules. At school those rules are followed. You know that. We never use vulgar language at school. We think it is good for you to speak politely and properly because that prevents problems here at school or anywhere else.
>
> We want you to be your best and that includes speaking wisely to show what a smart, helpful, and friendly person you can be. You know the punishment for breaking this rule, so you will write a two-page paper on why it is important to follow the rule about no vulgar language and you will clean the classroom every day for a week.
>
> That community service means you do something good to make up for doing something bad. Of course, you also will apologize to the other student for your vulgar language you used toward him. After class I will listen to that apology, which will include sincerely saying something friendly and positive to him.

The teacher did not criticize the brother or the father. The teacher did not comment that the father probably did not suggest use of vulgar language. The teacher did include a tactful statement that obeying the school rule has benefits at school and beyond school. The teacher did not accept the student's explanation as sufficient; rather, the teacher emphasized that the student's vulgarity was wrong, the student would be punished, and the student would make amends.

There are many predictable situations that middle school educators will encounter involving middle school students. Why study theories of learning or theories of human growth and development as preparation for working in a middle school when reality governs the school? The creators of those theories often are not working day-to-day in the middle school arena; rather, they are far, in miles and in years, from the middle school reality.

How does a theory from someone who never taught middle school or who has not worked in a middle school for many years, possibly decades, provide the specific, realistic, right-now practicality that the very active and immediate work of a middle school teacher requires? Abandon the theories. Emphasize the exact, specific, proven actions that get results. We know what works. Emphasize the actions that work.

A middle school English classroom has some 6th graders with outstanding reading and writing skills, a larger group with quite ordinary reading and writing skills, plus a third group of several students whose reading and writing skills are far below 6th grade level. What is the teacher to do, apply a theory or take certain action?

A 7th grade math class is doing work that has some complexity, but is well within the computational skills and the math reasoning skills that 7th graders should have. About half of the class is making great progress with the word problems while the other half is generally unable or unwilling to figure out what the problems require. What is the teacher to do? Apply a theory or take certain action?

The 8th grade science teacher used a carefully prepared test with forty multiple choice questions and one essay question. Two versions of the test were used, although both versions had the same questions. The sequence of the multiple choice questions was changed so students who cheated by copying another student's answers would be obvious from their incorrect answers. The results show that two students clearly cheated. What is the teacher to do? Apply a theory or take certain action?

Three 7th graders are creating unusual and offensive sketches in their art class. Within seconds the tranquility of the class is shattered as these three students begin to argue, threaten each other, push each other, and then one student grabs the sketches of the other two students and destroys their drawings. What is the teacher to do? Apply a theory or take certain action?

A middle school assistant principal reads a discipline referral about an 8th grader who repeatedly disobeyed exact instructions to not talk, to stay seated in the desk, and to complete the assignment that everyone was doing. What is the assistant principal to do? Apply a theory or take certain action?

A middle school counselor is dealing with eight 7th graders who have divided into two groups who tease each other, bully each other, and verbally abuse each other, and this has escalated into vicious text cyber attacks on each other. This problem began with some situation at a party over the weekend and now it is harming the school on Monday. The counselor gets the eight students into two different offices and asks the principal to help resolve this. What are the counselor and the principal to do? Apply a theory or take certain action?

The author of this book would answer each question above with "take certain action." "Certain" means precise, exact, swift—not immediate, not as an emotional reaction, but as a thoughtful, measured, direct, consistent-with-policy problem-solving approach—and serious. Discipline includes punishment and redirection. The misbehavior must be punished. The student or students who misbehaved must be redirected toward proper conduct through efforts that challenge the student and equip the student to think better and to behave better. Theories do not discipline students. Clear and certain actions are more effective.

"But don't actions need to be based on some overall theory or philosophy or standards?" That is a reasonable question because ideally every action at a middle school consistently moves the school closer to fulfilling its purpose, which is to cause learning. The school's curriculum states what is to be learned in each subject or class at each grade level. The complete curriculum can include what is to be learned and achieved in academic classes, what is to be learned and achieved regarding proper behavior, and what is to be learned and experienced through extracurricular participation.

The curriculum is implemented through the many actions taken daily by faculty, administration, counselors, and staff as they work with students. The curriculum is the overall objective of the school, but it is not a vague or broad philosophy and theory. The curriculum states what is to be accomplished. The certain actions taken minute-to-minute by middle school educators implement the curriculum.

It is proper action in middle school that generates desired results. Theories or philosophies are interesting, sophisticated, fascinating, perhaps lofty; however, working at a middle school is not theoretical or philosophical. Working at a middle school is real. To work at a middle school is to be continuously face-to-face with reality. Abandon the theories. Know what actions work and be able to create new actions, as needed, that work.

With that emphasis on action, what should college preparation programs for middle school educators provide? Experiences, knowledge, know-how that equip the future middle school educator to take the actions that get good results with middle school students individually and collectively. The perspective of some survey participants will provide further insights below.

One very relevant survey statement for participants to ponder was, "College programs that prepare people to work in middle schools must . . ."

- "Strengthen the content knowledge of pre-service teachers. Know how to utilize technology. Educate pre-service teachers on literacy strategies."

- "College programs must prepare future teachers as well as possible for long days, dealing with unrealistic parents, and working with administrators who are short on recent experience."
- "Remind future middle school teachers of the raging hormones and emotions with this age student."
- "Stress the importance of building relationships and utilizing effective communication with students and families. Also, stress the professional code of conduct."
- "Give them chances to go into a middle school often and get to know all about the setting. No book or paper can teach that like experiencing it can."
- "Stress the uniqueness of the students and how to differentiate instruction based on the student's academic needs."
- "Do a better job of screening personalities. Successful middle school teachers need a certain and different demeanor to work with middle schoolers and their needs."
- "Give them actual experience. College classroom instruction is important, but the most valuable information comes from being with students and implementing what you are learning in the college classroom."
- "Visit many different middle schools."

Notice there are zero references to theories or philosophies. These expert and experienced middle school practitioners emphasize action.

Another very relevant statement on the survey addressing college preparation programs for future middle school educators said, "The advice I would give to people who teach in those college programs is . . ." The responses follow.

- "Become involved with partnering with middle schools to develop relationships with students and staff."
- "Visit high-performing middle schools."
- "For those who teach in college programs, I would suggest substitute teaching for a week every year. Teachers have early bus duty, hundreds of interactions throughout the day, teaching 140 students, late bus duty, game duty to help supervise a sports event, then home to grade papers for another three hours. Observing a class or walking through the halls once a semester cannot quite give a true picture of a middle school teacher's job."
- "Be in tune with the middle school student, with changes in academic demands on middle schools, and with the influence of technology on students at school and away from school."
- "Get your students into various middle schools, both those with great reputations and those that are struggling."

- "Have, create, and implement courses with realistic tools and strategies to be used with middle school students."
- "Role play and teach conflict resolution. Include a legal issues course."
- "Share realistic examples of what teachers can expect to face in the middle school environment."
- "Talk more about building relationships, classroom management, academic needs, and learning styles."
- "Get into the classroom and teach middle schoolers again, not for a day, but a month or as a long-term substitute teacher. Try it in a school with a high percentage of free and reduced lunches and in a different school with a low percentage of free and reduced lunches."
- "Let us at middle schools know what you need college students to have learned and to be able to do by the time they finish high school."
- "Be realistic with the college students."
- "Require college students to work in the classroom more before student teaching."

Relationships. Reality. Practicality. Authenticity. Experience. Know the content that will be taught. Know how to manage a classroom. Know a variety of teaching methods, techniques, and activities. Spend a lot of time in middle schools.

The qualitative survey had a limited number of participants, yet no participant suggested more theories and philosophies. Why study theory after theory and philosophy after philosophy only to realize that doing the job of a middle school educator well is about taking the right action in the right way at the right time.

Of course, it is interesting to know some of the theories, philosophies, constructs, and concepts of human growth and development; however, Monday morning at a middle school is not a concept or a theoretical model. Monday morning at a middle school is pure reality, as are the other times on Monday and on each day.

Middle school students are not philosophical models. Middle school students are real people living real lives in the midst of the middle school maze right now. There is no hypothetical, theoretical, or philosophical path through the middle school maze. The maze is traveled one step at a time, one very realistic step at a time.

The entrance of the middle school maze could validly feature large signs that state, "This is a theory-free zone. Actions are our foundation, strength, and answer. Proper actions will get you through the maze safely, securely, productively and successfully, as you are guided, directed, corrected, and encouraged by capable educators who know all about the maze. Team up with these educators and you will conquer the maze. Reject or resist these educators and you give the maze an unnecessary advantage. Work with us and the advantages will be yours."

How does a college program prepare a twenty-year-old college junior to become a middle school teacher? Make sure that the college student masters the content knowledge of the subject or subjects that will be taught in middle school. A future middle school math teacher must know math as well as a college junior who majors in math. Perhaps majoring in the subject or subjects to be taught should be required.

Make sure that the future middle school math teacher knows every proven method of teaching every middle school math skill. It is not good enough to know a way to teach math. During a school year a middle school math teacher will encounter scholars who seek a challenge and at-risk students who need to work on addition, subtraction, multiplication, and division. Know many ways and be capable of creating more ways to teach math so each student learns the required math and more.

Make sure that the future middle school teacher spends much time in middle schools being as involved as possible. This time is a crucial reality check that can affirm the career decision to teach middle school or that can reveal that another career would be a better choice.

Make sure that the future middle school teacher masters the arts of people skills, work ethic, and relationship building. Working at a school means interacting with people nonstop during each day. From exemplary manners whenever possible to uncompromising toughness whenever necessary, the future middle school teacher must be ready to shift from one role to another. A theater class can be helpful to learn "acting for everyday use" so in those situations where you must deal with a student or a colleague in ways that are not using your dominant personality traits, you can shift into the role that is required at that moment.

Create opportunities for future middle school teachers to work with middle school students as tutors, mentors, and volunteer teaching assistants in properly supervised, wholesome ways. College students who aspire to be journalists write for the college newspaper or announce for the college radio station. Those practical experiences help build skills or help show that this work is not the best choice.

College students who would become middle school teachers need to experience as fully as possible the real work of middle school teaching so a good match is confirmed, a bad match is realized, or a maybe match gets the serious attention needed to improve if improvement is possible.

When necessary, say no. College programs that prepare future middle school teachers need to say no to some applicants. Not everyone is suited to teach. Not everyone who is capable of teaching is suited to teach middle school. Middle school educators need to be true believers in the work of middle school, in their commitment to that work, and in their dedication to middle school students.

Teaching middle school cannot be seen as a task that is a fall-back, Plan B, "something to do until I get a better opportunity." College programs can say no to applicants who do not convince the middle school educator selection participants that they are serious, dedicated, willing to work, eager to learn, and single-mindedly devoted to middle school teaching.

Middle school educator programs in colleges must make sure that professors know the reality of middle school teaching today. Last decade's methods and last year's lectures may have worked then, but reality is updated continuously. Today's 7th graders are not identical to last year's 7th graders or to last decade's 7th graders, and the differences are greater when contrasted with last generation's 7th graders.

Middle school educators will gladly tell college professors of future middle school teachers what needs to be known and what is not useful. Ask them. Invite them to your classes. Go to their classrooms. Get the college students into those middle school classrooms.

Arrange the college class schedules of would-be middle school teachers so they can substitute teach one day per week during their junior year of college. They will get paid in money and in new awareness of the middle school reality, adventure, and maze.

Their reactions could range from "I can't wait to teach middle school" to "I'm changing my major tomorrow from middle school teacher to something else." Either conclusion is good for the college student, for middle school students of the future, and for other careers that will receive newly inspired former would-be middle school teachers.

What do college and universities that have graduate school programs for future middle school principals and assistant principals need to provide and need to omit? Begin with what is not needed and that is theories or philosophies, concepts or constructs.

"But isn't there a comprehensive middle school philosophy that shows the differences between a middle school and the old junior high? Wouldn't that be a helpful philosophy to know?"

That is a reasonable question, but it is not the most important question and it may be a distraction. There is an idea of a middle school that is different than the idea of a junior high school. The middle school idea centers more on the reality of work with eleven- to fourteen-year-olds in the realistic here and now. The junior high school idea centers more on the future reality of high school and concentrating on preparing eleven- to fourteen-year-olds for when they will be high school students.

Future middle school administrators need to know the management and leadership actions that help make a middle school fully achieve its purpose, which is to cause learning of the entire curriculum by each student. Similar to middle school teachers, only the very serious, very dedicated, very capable, very willing-to-work-at-a-nonstop-pace-all-day-each-day, very knowledgeable, very conscientious, and very caring should consider this endeavor of middle school administration.

Middle school principals or assistant principals work in the same building as middle school teachers, yet the jobs are vastly different; however, reality still guides what needs to be known, what needs to be done, and how that needs to be done. It is again necessary to abandon the theories.

There are many interesting theories of and concepts of leadership. These approaches may come with unique nomenclature, new slogans, clever, trendy words, charts, graphics, blueprints, and schematics.

There are many interesting theories of and concepts of management. These approaches also may come with unique terminology, creative slogans, cute, trendy words, detailed charts, colorful graphics, precise blueprints, and trendy schematics.

Some of these leadership and management theories, concepts, trends, or fads are designed for business, for corporations, for entrepreneurs. The business arena is different from the middle school arena. Leadership and management methods that get good results in the business world may not work at all in a middle school where most people are eleven to fourteen years old and where all adult workers have chosen a career that is not in a business.

Just as future middle school teachers need to be taught the reality of middle school and the many possible actions that can get good results in middle school classrooms, future middle school administrators need to be taught the reality of middle school leadership and management. Those future principals and assistant principals also need to be taught the many possible actions that can get good results in the multiple responsibilities that are included in the job description of a middle school administrator.

We know what works in middle school teaching. Just ask great middle school teachers and they will tell you. Watch a lot of great middle school teachers and they will show you. Recall what your best middle school teachers did and those memories will inform you. Recall what your other middle school teachers did or did not do and those memories will further guide you.

The recollections of what your middle school administrators did will be very limited because most middle school students see very little of what their school administrators do. So go ask current middle school administrators about their work. Seek superior principals and assistant principals who can provide insights. Notice closely what the administrators of your school do and how they do it. Keep a promise list, which is what you promise yourself you will do for the middle school of which you become an administrator.

Graduate school programs that enable educators to earn certification as middle school administrators need to abandon the theories and, instead, emphasize the realities. Current and recently retired middle school administrators could advise professors, could be guest speakers, or could teach a class. These people could add perspective about what makes middle school leadership and management unique.

Be practical. If a course is required in school finance, emphasize the actual money management, bookkeeping, legal requirements, actual school district procedures, common mistakes and how to prevent them, rather than esoteric contemplation of various tax concepts to pay for public education. Middle school principals do not set tax rates. Middle school principals work with colleagues to allocate funds and account for funds at the school level. Teach more financial realities that actually occur daily as part of the middle school administrator's job.

Parents get irate. Neighbors of the school have complaints. A teacher is absent Friday after Friday and is late most Mondays. A custodian does half of the job and expects all of the pay. School will dismiss two hours early due to bad weather. No fire drill was conducted last month.

Teacher evaluations are due in three weeks. Two 7th graders just got into a fight a few minutes after two 8th graders got into a fight. The superintendent has many questions about test scores, school supervision, and student attendance at the school. Higher-than-normal teacher turnover means ten positions to fill instead of the usual four or five.

Those circumstances are reality in middle school. Some of those and more could happen on any day. It can feel like a perpetual emergency (see Babbage, *911: The School Administrator's Guide to Crisis Management*; Rowman & Littlefield Education, 1996). We know what works in middle school administration. Superior middle school principals and assistant principals show what works daily. Ask them. Invite them. Team up with them. Put their knowledge and experience into the graduate school program for future middle school administrators.

The author spent thirteen fascinating years as a middle school administrator. There are no recollections of times when theories were the answer to a question or the solution to a problem. What mattered was making the right decision, taking the right action in the right way, constantly interacting with people, preventing problems whenever possible, being in classrooms, being in hallways, being in the cafeteria, talking to people, rewarding great work, rewarding improvement, knowing and following policies and laws, getting advice, giving encouragement, punishing when necessary, rewarding when possible. No theories. Much action. That's the job. That's the reality.

Lofty, esoteric, conceptual, theoretical classes about idealistic models of leadership and management are not the way to prepare future middle school administrators. Teach them the realities of the job. Show them what great middle school administrators are doing now. Involve them in administrator preparation duties at a middle school such as being the chair of a school committee, being a teaching team leader, being on a school improvement committee.

Future teachers of middle school students and future administrators of middle schools need to fully know the reality of middle school, not theories, and need to know the most useful actions to implement with every possible situation that can arise. The college or graduate school curriculum and experience for these future middle school experts needs to be based on reality and action, just as middle school itself is.

Chapter Seven

Middle School Students

My name is Janet. I'm in the 6th grade. I'm supposed to tell you about 6th grade.

Well, I don't like 6th grade very much. I like 5th grade a lot better. Fifth grade was, you know, it was really neat. We did a lot of fun stuff in 5th grade. We took some trips to a museum and a park. That was fun.

The other best thing in 5th grade was I had always gone to that school since I was five years old and in kindergarten. I went to the same elementary school. I knew everyone and I knew all about the school.

Sixth grade is different. It's a big place—I mean, the school building is really big. We started school a month ago and sometimes I still feel lost. I can pretty much find my classes, but I don't know any other place. Well, I know where the cafeteria is and where the library is. But I don't know anything about the 7th grade or 8th grade areas.

Speaking of 7th graders and 8th graders, I knew some of them from elementary school, but they never speak to me. They never speak to any 6th graders. They think they are better than us, I guess. They must think they're just too cool to talk to a 6th grader.

My teachers are really strict. We had a test in every class about the rules, school rules, team rules, classroom rules. All we heard the first week was rules.

I'm on the Challengers team. There are six teachers on the team. They teach my classes—English, math, science, social studies, Spanish, and reading. I know how to read, so that class is dumb. All we do in math is stuff I already know. Spanish is really hard.

I also take art class and I'm in the orchestra so I take that class. I want to quit orchestra because I never liked it. My family made me learn to play the violin when I was in 4th grade. They said I had to keep playing violin this year. They thought I'd like it more in middle school. Wrong.

Art class is cool. We do stuff every day. I want to take art all year, but we change those classes in January. Why not let me take it all year if I like it so much? Middle school does things like that to you. They make you do stuff you hate and they don't let you do stuff you like.

There's another 6th grade team, the Seekers. My best friends are on that team. I asked my math teacher if I could move to that team. He said to talk to my counselor. She said no. I told my parents and they said for me to do my best on the Challengers team.

All I want is to quit orchestra, take more art, and move to the other team. I'm not allowed to do any of that. Now you know why I don't like 6th grade.

There are other reasons. I said that 7th and 8th graders never talk to 6th graders. Well, they talk *about* us. You hear them in the halls making mean comments about 6th graders. They tease us for being new or lost or little or other stuff. That's no fun. One day I pretended to be sick so I would not have to come to school because one 8th grader was mean to me the day before.

I don't even know that 8th grader. She just started yelling at me in the halls and she yelled at my friends. I told a teacher and I think the girl got sent to the office. But I still wonder if she is going to bother us again.

I might try out for the girls' basketball team. I like basketball. But my grades are not great so far. We just got our first progress report and my grades were nothing like they were in 5th grade. I always made good grades. When my parents saw a D grade in math and another D in science they went crazy.

My other grades were A or B. Math is dumb. I know everything we are doing so I do well on tests, but the homework or work in class is dumb and I don't always turn it in.

I don't know about science. The teacher is new. She seems confused, and she's been absent a lot so we had substitutes. I think my grade is a C or a B in science, but the teacher has not put our last two tests in the computer yet. I did great on those tests, I know I did, but we still don't have them back so what can I tell my parents?

So, I don't like 6th grade. My friends don't like it either. My cousin goes to another middle school and he's in 6th grade. He loves 6th grade. He tells me about his neat classes and the new stuff they learn about. He said they are already doing 7th grade math work. He also said that 7th and 8th graders can take art all year long. Maybe I should go to his school.

One more thing. My best friend in the 6th grade has this boyfriend. He's in the 6th grade. She never talks to me anymore. They've liked each other for a week or maybe two weeks. So I don't have a best friend any more. That's another reason I don't like 6th grade.

* * *

My real name is Nathaniel. My mom and dad call me Nathan. My friends call me Nate. I'm in the 7th grade.

I thought 7th grade would be better than 6th grade, but, well, you know, it's just the same old school stuff. Not much is different. At least I'm not one of the lost 6th graders any more. 6th grade was awful. You have to get used to a new school. You have all these different teachers. There are all kinds of rules and stuff.

So how are my classes? Pretty boring. We do worksheets and we watch videos. My grades are OK. That's because the work is so easy. It's pretty much 6th grade all over again in math and in English. Science is sort of different, but not really new stuff.

I do have this really cool technology class. We work with computers and little robots and even a flight simulator. We never have worksheets there. We really do stuff.

What's really bad about 7th grade is the students who get in trouble all the time. They are so stupid. They got in trouble last year. They steal. They fight. They bully people. They lie. It's no fun with them here.

I actually asked one teacher why they don't send those students somewhere else. She had no answer and told me to get back to work. I think she should get to work and get rid of those really bad 7th graders. Why are they allowed to stay here?

Last year I played on the football team. Not this year. The coach was so unfair. He had his favorite players. Even if they missed practice or goofed off, they got to play in the games. I quit football. I might play again in high school.

The food at school is not so bad. They have pizza a lot. Lunch is too short. Why can't we go in the gym during lunch?

I decided to join the chess club. I don't know anything about chess, but there's this really pretty girl who is in that club and she does not know I exist. So I went to a chess club meeting and she talked to me, kind of. She talked to my friend and I stood there looking at her. I hope she likes me. I did learn something about chess. It's a neat game.

We had this really dumb assembly at school. It was supposed to tell us all about stupid stuff on the Internet. So we watched a video and then we heard a speaker. It was so dumb. I know more about the Internet than the speaker knows. These old people, you know he was probably like forty or fifty, try to be cool when they tell us about Internet crimes or stuff. We don't pay attention. I guess they have to tell us that stuff because I know some 8th graders who do awful computer things, but we still don't pay attention at assemblies like that.

My suggestion would be to have high school students tell us about Internet stuff. My older brother is an expert on that. He has a friend who got arrested for some crazy Internet hacking or something. I would pay attention to that. Nobody wants to go to jail.

Oh, yeah, speaking of jail, I know a 7th grader who is in juvenile jail. He stole a bunch of stuff from a store. Then he tried to sell the stuff. Then he went back to the same store and stole more, but the store manager stopped him and called the police. He is in so much trouble.

I know some other students here who do stupid stuff like that. There's a group here and they break into lockers and steal stuff. I really want to tell on them. Maybe I will. I've seen them steal. I'm just scared of what could happen to me if I told on them. I'm not sure what to do.

Well, that's about it. I hope that 8th grade is better, but it probably won't be. High school looks really cool. My brother and my sister are in high school. He's in the marching band and says it's really neat. She plays volleyball and loves it. They make good grades and they say that the classes are better than in middle school.

I wonder if I could skip 8th grade and go to high school next year. Maybe I'll ask about that. The answer will probably be no, but I'll ask. Why stay here another year?

* * *

My name is Katy. I'm in the 8th grade. I like school. I'm not crazy about school, but I like it. My friends are here. I work on the yearbook. I tutor 6th graders in math. I started a table tennis club last year and it's really fun. And I'm in the chorus. I love to sing. So, I like school, but I'm not crazy about school.

What I really like is soccer. I started playing when I was four, so I've played for almost ten years. My school does not have soccer, so I play for this really good team in a league. Everybody on the team is thirteen or fourteen years old. We've played together for a long time, since we were really little.

I make really good grades. I'm always on the Honor Roll. It's no big deal. I always turn in my work. It's so easy. I study for tests and I do what teachers tell us to do in class.

I want to go to college. My family cannot pay for college, so I have to get a lot of scholarships. I plan to make straight A's in high school and to play soccer. I'll do a bunch of other stuff so I get scholarships for everything there is.

The only thing 8th grade can do for me now is get me ready for high school. I have friends in 9th grade who say high school is really tough. Some of them did OK in middle school but are failing in 9th grade. I can't do that.

I'm kind of tired of middle school. There's so much stupid stuff. There's always some rumor or lie or stuff going on. I'm not perfect, but I stay out of trouble. Some people here are always in trouble. I get sick of them.

We have this new teacher in science this year. Every day we do some experiment or laboratory work. It's really neat to see that stuff. Last year in science we just used the book. This year we never use the book. For the first time I like science.

Math is different. All we do is problems from the book. My soccer coach keeps all kinds of statistics about our games, even our practices. Soccer math is really interesting. School math is always so boring. Why can't we do soccer math at school, or basketball math or, who knows, paying for college math?

Maybe the teachers should ask us sometimes what we want to learn. Our science teacher knows I play soccer. She brought a soccer ball to class and a baseball, a basketball, and something else, oh yeah, a golf ball. We did these neat experiments with the sports equipment. There are reasons that a soccer ball is made a certain way. It was so interesting. Why can't we do stuff like that in all of our classes?

I went to a dance at school last Friday. It was OK, but I won't go again. The boys act silly. Maybe the girls were silly, but what's the point of just running around or just sitting there or talking about somebody else. The music wasn't very good. Some teachers planned the dance. Maybe they should have asked us what we like at a dance. It doesn't matter. I tried it and it was no good. I can find better things to do.

There was this one boy at the dance. He's really cute. He talked to me for a long time and then he danced with some other girl. He never talked to me again. Stupid boys. That's another reason to never go to another dance at school.

So, you know, 8th grade is going pretty well. I can't wait to get to high school. I'm going to make great grades and I really want my high school to win the state soccer championship. Some of the girls on my soccer team will go to high school with me. We talk about being state champs a lot. So that's what I look forward to, finishing 8th grade and going to high school so I can earn scholarships for college. And keep playing soccer.

I'm starting to like science. Maybe I can study science a lot in high school and get scholarships that way. I wonder if anybody here knows anything about that. I'll ask my science teacher. She's my best teacher.

I do have one other question. I get free breakfast and free lunch at school now. I think I'll get that in high school. Do college scholarships pay for food? Or do I have to earn money for that? I need to find out about that.

Thomas Columbia loves 7th grade. He loved 6th grade and he loved elementary school. Thomas knew how to read before he started school. As a young child his family taught him the alphabet, how to count, and some advanced vocabulary.

Thomas has always done more than is required. At school, he always has a book or two checked out from the school library. He participates in his middle school's WORD program, which stands for Wonderful Opportunities for Reading Daily. Students who commit to this program may come to the library before school starts in the morning, after they finish lunch, and after school.

Students in the WORD program are required to read at least two books per month. They also take a test on each book they read and must score 90% or better on the test. When a student has read five, then ten, then fifteen, and then twenty books, there are rewards given. The rewards come from a local bookstore and include books, front row seats at events with authors, and free admission to writing workshops the store arranges for local authors to teach.

Thomas's family is very involved with running. His father was on the track team in college and his mother ran cross-country in college. Thomas has an older brother who is on the high school track team and an older sister who is on the high school cross-country team.

Thomas prefers cross-country to track, although he is on the middle school track team. There is not a cross-country team at the middle school, but next year as an 8th grader Thomas will be allowed to run on the high school cross-country team.

So, Thomas does very well in school, never gets in trouble, turns in all his work on time, and is involved with school activities. There is only one problem that Thomas has found repeatedly, but the problem never has been fully solved until this year.

Science has always been quite difficult for Thomas. He does the work and he makes good grades in science, but learning science takes twice the effort of any other subject for Thomas. Not any more. It all changed with 7th grade science.

Mr. Emmanuel is Thomas's 7th grade science teacher. Before class began one day early in Thomas's 7th grade year Mr. Emmanuel heard Thomas talking about some serious bicycle riding Thomas had been doing as part of a new cross-training program for the track team.

Track is a spring sport at Thomas's school and the track team begins their official work on March 15. The track coach gave all interested students, track team participants or not, information about exercise, training, nutrition, and fitness. Thomas read all of that and created his own personal fitness plan for the August through March time period.

Mr. Emmanuel heard Thomas talking about fitness in general and about bicycle riding in particular. He asked Thomas, "Do you know how much science goes into making a bicycle? How about the science of riding a bicycle in the most efficient way?"

Thomas was surprised by the idea that science, a subject he did not much like and always had to work extra hard with, could have anything to do with bicycling, which is an activity that Thomas likes a lot and is good at. "Science and bicycles. I would never think they had anything to do with each other. How's that work, Mr. Emmanuel?"

The perfect question. Mr. Emmanuel saw a great teaching opportunity. "Thomas, let's answer that question. I'll find some articles and some video material about bicycles and science, even about how bicycles are made and about aerodynamics. You can read those. Then I'll talk to people at a bicycle shop. I'd like for you to assemble a bicycle. If you put a bike together you'll see and touch the science. Then you could tell the class all about it."

The results surpassed Mr. Emmanuel's highest hopes. Thomas and science became very good friends. Thomas read the articles about bicycles and science. He was also interested in an article about the history of bicycles. His social studies teacher was impressed when Thomas added that insight to a discussion on the history of transportation in the late nineteenth century.

Thomas was fascinated with the task of assembling a bicycle. Mr. Emmanuel arranged for Thomas to visit with the owners of a local bicycle shop. Thomas's father went on that visit and it became a meaningful father and son outing. Thomas asked the owner about working there at the bicycle shop in a few years. The owner encouraged Thomas to apply for a job as soon as he was sixteen years old. The owner also said that Thomas had to make all A or B grades in high school to be considered for a job.

Thomas was so inspired by the bicycle activity and adventure that science became a class he always eagerly anticipated. Mr. Emmanuel had found a perfect way to connect Thomas's dedication to running, fitness, and bicycling with 7th grade science. The imagination and energy of Thomas, a previously science-resistant student, was now applied to make Thomas a science achiever in particular and more of a middle school achiever in general.

There is no one perfectly and precisely representative middle school student whose personality and academic profile exemplifies all middle school students. Janet, Nathaniel, Katy, and Thomas are four unique middle school students who share some of the overall characteristics of and proclivities of middle school students yet who also have genuine, unduplicated individuality. For middle school educators who embrace the adventure of discovering student individuality combined with knowing the overall tendencies and characteristics of middle school students in general, the experience of working with 6th, 7th, and 8th graders can be very fertile for enhancing academic achievement and personal growth in students. There can also be much professional achievement, growth, meaning, and rewards for middle school educators who are so inclined.

My name is Nicole. I am an 8th grader at Stevenson Middle School. Our school is named for a lady who was a teacher and then principal for a long time. When we were 6th graders we read this little biography about Ms. Angela Stevenson. She worked her way through college, became a teacher, and then was a principal of another middle school. I think she worked in schools for something like thirty-five years.

I don't see how she kept doing this stuff for so long. Why would anybody finish middle school and high school, then go to college, and, you know, then work in a school forever. Me, I want to finish school and never come back.

I started thinking about that on the first day of 8th grade. My English teacher had us write some dumb paper on the very first day of school. It was about what we want to be when we grow up. Who knows?

My first idea was to say I want to be far away from middle school. You know, this school stuff gets old. So far, 8th grade is a lot like 6th and 7th grade—classes, books, homework, tests, rules, report cards, more homework. The same stuff every year. So, I decided to do something different with my English paper.

My answer was one word—me. I want to be me when I grow up. I'd like to be me right now, but I'm about halfway through 8th grade, so I have to be an 8th grader. I have to do all of this school stuff. That's not me. I know school is important. My parents tell me that all the time. I just don't get interested in school. It's always the same stuff.

There is something else that I am interested in. I like to cook. I'm a really good cook. A few years ago I got to spend several days with my grandparents at Thanksgiving. My grandmother, she's my mother's mother, is a great cook. She started fixing everything for Thanksgiving on Tuesday. I had no idea it took two days to fix everything.

She let me help. We baked pies. We cooked green beans. We did everything to prepare a turkey and ham, then we cooked both of them. She showed me how to cook cranberries and how to make a fancy sweet potato casserole. We made biscuits and rolls and cornbread.

I asked my grandmother why we didn't just go to a restaurant and let them do the work. She said it was no work at all to do the cooking for her family at Thanksgiving. She loved doing all that. No restaurant could match her cooking, she told me. Plus, she likes to have all of the family at her home on Thanksgiving.

I helped clean everything after our big Thanksgiving meal. Then my grandmother showed me how to make turkey soup, turkey hash, and how to get all of the meat off of the turkey, not just the slices. Ever since then, I've learned a lot more about cooking. I help cook at my house. I think I could be a real cook, you know, a chef. Why can't I learn about that at school?

So, I'm sort of stuck in the 8th grade. I have some friends. My grades are good enough to stay out of trouble. I behave pretty good. I just don't like school. My counselor told me that the school used to have a cooking class called home economics. They quit teaching it because they decided everyone is supposed to go to college, so we needed classes to prepare us for college.

I'm not going to college. I'm going to a cooking school. Maybe in high school I can take cooking classes. Maybe while I'm in high school I can work at a restaurant, even fast food would be some experience. As soon as I get out of middle school maybe I can start doing stuff I care about. I've had enough math and science and stuff like that.

School always tells us what to do. Why can't my science project be about cooking? Why can't my math work be about recipes? Why can't the book I read for English class be about food and cooking and, you know, restaurants or things like that? Why can't I just be me and do what I care about?

My grandmother never made me do math and science when we cooked everything for Thanksgiving, but we did have to measure things and that oven really got hot. I even called some company to ask a question about checking the temperature of a turkey. They said I asked a really good question. My teachers never say that. You know why? Nobody asks good questions about school stuff. Come on, what is there that is worth asking about short stories or square roots. School stuff is pretty stupid.

How could Nicole's fascination with cooking be applied to middle school work? What could be done with her class assignments to connect math, science, social studies, language arts, health, physical education, art, and other classes? Could there be a cooking club? Could Nicole spend some time with the cafeteria staff to learn from them?

Could Nicole's teaching team identify the wholesome interest of each 8th grader they teach and create academic activities that connect the curriculum with those interests? Can middle school be a highly productive blend of academic challenges, academic achievement, and simultaneous self-discovery? Could that combination of experiences help show Nicole what she can become as an 8th grader, as a high school student, and as a cook?

Some thoughts on questions like those can be provided by an experienced middle school teacher. Katlyn Bancroft has taught middle school for seventeen years. She and her husband, Tim, are the parents of thirteen-year-old twin daughters, Marian and Martha, who are in 7th grade. Mrs. Bancroft is known for her very well managed, very highly structured, very creative, and very productive classroom. Her students learn the middle school math curriculum. They also learn about themselves and about life. Katlyn expresses her knowledge this way.

> I learned years ago that 6th graders are different than 7th graders and that 8th graders are different than 6th or 7th graders. I also learned that each student is unique, individual, one of a kind. Sure, they have some overall similarities, but there are no two identical middle school students.
>
> Sometimes I think I've seen everything that can happen in a middle school, but then something new happens. It might be something new that is good or something new that is a concern. Recently an 8th grader at this school asked me to sponsor a club she wanted to start. It's an investment club. There are about ten students who would like to create virtual investments and compete in a stock market game.
>
> That request was new to me. I said yes and the group has had three meetings already. They research companies. They have arranged for a stockbroker to be a guest speaker at a meeting. They are really serious. I'm impressed. When I was in 8th grade I never thought about money or investing the way these students do.
>
> Then there is another new group at our school. It meets in the evening once each month. This group is for grandparents who have guardian responsibility for a grandchild who is in our middle school. At most meetings there are twenty to thirty people attending and the number continues to increase.
>
> Bless their hearts, these dear grandparents are sixty to seventy years old or so and now they have full responsibility for rearing a twelve-year-old. The meetings are very productive. They share ideas. Experts come to speak. Our school counselors give great advice at the meetings. Earlier in my career there just was not a need for this type of support group. The need for this group increases every year.

People ask me what has changed with students during the seventeen years I have been a teacher. In some ways, not very much. In other ways, a lot. Middle school students have always had a good supply of curiosity and energy. They like to be active. If you connect with them, if they know you will go the extra mile for them, they will go extra miles for you.

But there is the reality that some middle school students are court involved. Maybe I was too idealistic, but when I was preparing to become a teacher I never thought about what would need to be done with a student who was arrested, placed in juvenile jail, and then eventually came back to school.

I had to file charges against a student two years ago. He became out of control in my classroom. He threw things. He used awful language. He broke the window in the door when he slammed it repeatedly. He put everyone in danger. The police were called. He was charged with disorderly conduct because even with the police here he continued to be out of control until they put handcuffs on him. I never expected to see anything like that.

Most of the students do what they are supposed to do most of the time. About 90 percent of the behavior problems at this school are caused by about 5 percent of the students. That group hates school. They have been through every discipline action or academic intervention. They need to be in a vocational education program.

They could succeed in a job training program and it would do them so much more good than another year of failing regular classes. It was a noble idea for everyone to attend college, but it is so unrealistic. Truth is, it's not fair. There are many students who have other skills or career interests besides what college prepares you for.

I do think that the adults have to be in charge. We care deeply about the students. We try to apply their strengths and their interests to what we study. We find ways to utilize their energy and curiosity and sense of adventure. But the adults have to determine the curriculum and how the teaching is going to be done. We set the rules and we enforce the rules. I want the school to be student-friendly, but that does not mean fun and games. It means working and learning and behaving.

We need to do a lot more for the many, many students who do work and learn and behave. It is not fair for disruptive students or failing students to get so much extra attention or extra effort or second and third chances while the serious students do not get the opportunities and challenges they deserve.

I know we have to keep working with those students who don't care about school or who have already given up or who come here just to cause trouble. I really think that the most severe of them need to have an alternative school somewhere else. They would do better there. Then everyone else would benefit from fewer disruptions and things like that. The good students have rights, too.

So, I'm determined and confident. I come to school every day intending to get good results. The job is a lot more demanding now. Society expects schools to perform miracles. Every problem that children or teenagers have, schools are supposed to solve. It would be better if we could just concentrate on teaching instead of every action that politicians or vocal citizens think school should be used for. I am still optimistic, but I'm not so sure I would recommend teaching to a college student who is considering various career options.

Why? Because no matter how hard I work or how many hours I work, it is never enough. There's so much more stuff that teachers have to do now. Meetings to attend. Special accommodations for many individual students, some who need real help and appreciate it, but others are playing the political game that their parent or guardian set up by loud complaints and threats of a lawsuit. It's a tough job. If I could just be left to teach, it would be better. It used to be like that.

One more thought about the students. They are the best part of this work. When a teacher's efforts result in students really learning, it is very rewarding and very meaningful. That still happens a lot, but it is harder and harder to make it happen.

Something is different with students today. I wonder sometimes if it is all the hours they spend on cell phones or playing video games. I think you have to read, really read, to learn. I don't mean read gossip on social media. I mean read books, challenging books, creative books, biographies, literature, and great stories.

Then there's work ethic. Some students are so willing to work. They have that habit of expecting themselves to do every assignment on time and correctly. Others just do enough to get by and then others do close to nothing. What do those students expect? How did they get this far if they never do any work? How can I reverse their refusal to work and their reluctance to learn?

Then I see those lazy students before school or after school on their cell phones. Why would their family let them have a cell phone and waste hours with texting when the same student never even spends minutes on homework or reading?

Something else about students really concerns me. I blame television and movies and popular music and vulgar celebrities for this. It's the language and the rudeness. These students are eleven years old or twelve, thirteen, maybe fourteen, and their language is awful. It wasn't always like that. Not all of the students, but more of them than there used to be. In the hallways, at athletic events, even in the classroom, they use crude or vulgar language. I deal with it in my classroom. It is rare here in my room, but it should never happen.

I think popular culture and technology gadgets mislead the young people today. Some entertainer or athlete makes millions of dollars, breaks laws, talks trash, stuff like that, and students imitate it because they see it on television or somewhere. It sure makes our job more difficult as our society gets more crude and more rude. That's a terrible example for students. How do I fight the impact of pop culture?

Well, these students can accomplish so much. I'm still determined to do my best every day, but so much has changed over the years. I'm really concerned that this generation is getting lazy and sloppy. Not all of them, but more than there used to be. They can do so much better. They can be so much better. I can't give up on them, but this really is not the job I expected years ago and it's not the job I used to do ten or fifteen years ago.

I used to spend almost all of my time on teaching. Back then, fifteen years ago it was all about teaching. Now, I'm required to compensate for whatever is keeping any student from academic success. Well, if the student cannot read or if the student sleeps in class every day or if the student is court involved or if the student's parent makes endless excuses for the student or if the student starts a fight and gets suspended, what can I do? If some doctor claims the student has some vague syndrome that really is not proven, but it is one more excuse for not working and I make every required accommodation but the student refuses to do her part, what else can I do?

Or if a student keeps playing with his cell phone in class and I have already taken it away three times, turned it in at the office, and the student had no punishment, what else can I do?

Or if the state government changes the annual testing system in schools, but really can't give any clear direction about what the new tests will be like, how do I prepare lessons for the students and how do I get them ready for these new tests? Then in four or five years the state will change the tests again and everything I do will have to be done differently not because it is good for students, but because of politics and some mandates from people who really are out of touch with schools.

I just think we have done our students a real disservice by making school way too easy. Students are less willing to read, to study, to do homework, to behave, to follow rules, to be polite, so we are told to make adjustments and be sure that every student feels good about himself or herself. Well, a student who refuses to learn and who uses awful language and who never works should not feel good about any of that.

I just think that the students need some good old-fashioned basics, you know, reading, writing, arithmetic, spelling, memorizing, and discipline. We've become too politically correct and too soft. By thinking that no student should ever fail a class we've made classes too easy to pass. If society is going to mislead students about what is right and wrong, about what matters or what is not important, schools have to maintain the real standards of hard work, good manners, and obeying rules.

Students in middle school are just too young to know what classes to take or what decisions to make. I think school got sidetracked with some misguided social engineering or political correctness or bad psychology. I'm for hard work and strict rules because those work. I think we owe our students the truth and we owe them honesty. Life requires hard work and obeying rules. Life is not always fun and entertainment. School needs to be much more challenging and much more disciplined. That's what they need now, maybe more than ever.

Mrs. Bancroft's ideas, thoughts, and concerns are sincere. She is alarmed at declining trends she has noticed during her seventeen years of middle school teaching. She is determined, yet she is frustrated and troubled. No amount of extra hours invested into her work can fully reverse the descending trends she confronts each year. Yet, she is dedicated to doing great teaching for, with, and because of her students and due to her integrity.

Providing the best possible educational experience for middle school students is made possible by frequently and seriously listening to middle school teachers. Middle school teachers know today's middle school students, individually and collectively, better than anyone else involved in middle school education.

At a middle school, no person spends more time with middle school students than the teachers do. To most effectively address the needs of, the potential of, and the most productive learning opportunities for middle school students, increase the input of middle school teachers and increasingly base more decisions on that input.

The middle school teachers will not be the only source of input. Principals, assistant principals, counselors, other school staff members, parents and guardians, community members, students, policy makers, and lawmakers must be involved; however, weigh the impact of the various sources of input. Of all educators and of all people who seek to impact education, the most realistic input comes from the people who deal with the classroom reality and the student reality all day, every day. One essential way to improve the middle school experience for students is to increase the amount of and the use of input from teachers.

We hear now the words of Matthew Corinth, a high school senior. He is speaking at a ceremony for teachers who are retiring. For each of the twenty-six teachers in Matthew's school district who will retire at the end of the current school year, a student has been recruited to pay tribute to the teacher. Most of the students who will speak at the event are high school or middle school students, but a few are elementary school students. Matthew's comments follow.

My name is Matthew Corinth and in one month I will graduate from West Madison High School. I am here tonight to pay tribute to Mrs. Carolyn Boyle, my 7th grade English teacher. Mrs. Boyle will retire at the end of this school year after teaching for thirty-two years. She is the most inspiring, the most helpful, and the most important teacher I ever had.

Sixth grade was very difficult for me. My older sister had just finished middle school and everyone knew Paula Corinth. Paula made perfect grades, had perfect behavior, and had perfect attendance. She still does all of that in college and she did all of that in high school.

So my teachers in 6th grade called me Paula's brother as often as they called me Matthew. I could never ever live up to what Paula accomplished. I usually made good grades, I behaved pretty well, and I was rarely absent. Still, nothing I did was ever good enough for my teachers. They even told me sometimes, "You know, Paula never made a B" or "Paula was never absent."

OK. That was Paula. I wish I could be as smart and stuff as Paula, but I do have skills and talents and strengths and a different personality. I thought the teachers should let me be me, but they thought I should be just like Paula.

Then I finally got to 7th grade and I had Mrs. Boyle for English class. She never mentioned anyone's brother or sister for comparison or to get our attention. She asked about Paula once or twice, but she asked a lot more about me. She seemed to be glad to teach Matthew, not to teach Paula's brother.

Our first assignment in 7th grade English class was to write about what we hoped would be accomplished during the new school year. I wrote that I really wanted 7th grade to be the time when my teachers gave me a chance to be me. Well, Mrs. Boyle really liked that idea. She said that 7th grade English class was the perfect place for each student to be himself or herself.

She meant it. We read the best books. Usually we had lots of choices about what we read. I picked out books that were interesting to me. Mrs. Boyle insisted that we read the books, analyze the books, know the books, and really understand the books. I read seventeen books during 7th grade for that English class. That was more than we had to read, but Mrs. Boyle showed me that reading was really cool, so I read everything I could.

In high school I always read whatever was assigned, but I usually read more than that. Because of Mrs. Boyle I got interested in writing. I read all of those books and I thought I could write a book myself. I entered some writing contests in high school. I won five contests and two of them had college scholarships as prizes.

Speaking of college . . . the schools I applied to said my college essay was one of the best they ever read. The essay was all about how 7th grade English class with Mrs. Boyle made me the student I am now and helped me become fully ready for college. So, Mrs. Boyle, you are the best teacher I ever had. Congratulations on your retirement and on making so many students, including me, the young scholars we have become.

Matthew reveals how vital the middle school years are for each student. If the middle school years are filled with wise guidance, disciplined standards, challenging instruction, punishments when necessary, rewards when earned, encouragement when possible, and meaningful interaction continuously, the results are beneficial now and always. When we get the middle school years right, we establish a foundation upon which successful middle school students can build unlimited achievements with school in particular and with life in general. Maximizing the vital middle school years helps maximize the years that follow.

Chapter Eight

Middle School Curriculum, Academics, and Extracurricular Activities

What should the middle school curriculum be and what should it not be? What should the middle school curriculum do and not do? What should the middle school curriculum include and not include?

How is the academic program of a middle school best implemented? What predictable problems can be prevented and how are they prevented? What must be included in middle school academic methods and what should be excluded from middle school academic methods?

What instructional techniques work best with middle school students and what instructional techniques are unproductive or counterproductive in a middle school? Do the best instructional techniques vary for 6th graders, 7th graders, and 8th graders? Do the best instructional methods change from year to year, from generation to generation? Should instructional techniques change during a school year as 6th graders in August are not the same in January or April?

One source of answers to these questions is experienced middle school educators who are known for their expertise. These survey participants are such people. Their years of superior service have given them the wisdom that only time can provide. Their survey answers about middle school academics and curriculum were in response to the question, "On the academic side, what should the middle school curriculum include?"

- "A strong emphasis on standards-based curriculum with a wide elective offering."
- "Rigorous core classes, exploratory electives of year-long work, languages, music, orchestra and band classes."

- "The middle school curriculum should include an abundance of technology with more hands-on activities, not just running software packages or taking required tests via computer. A much wider variety of options should also be offered. Those sitting 'on the mountaintop' need to realize that not all students are going to college."
- "Real life experiences whenever possible."
- "A great variety of activities to cover all kinds of learning skills and learning styles."
- "Math, reading and writing, health, science, social studies, career exploration, service learning, arts and humanities, extracurricular opportunities."
- "They need exposure to different career path options."
- "Everything should have some real-life connection the students can make."
- "Options! Vocational training. Variety including physical education—maybe recess. Exploratory options that integrate math, language arts, and other core academic subjects."
- "The core content subjects, enriched exploratory classes, foreign language, technology curriculum."
- "Core content rigor that teaches to the highest level the students can obtain."
- "More real-world activities."

The areas of emphasis in the survey responses include: (A) real-world connections, (B) variety, (C) core academics, (D) many elective options, (E) career education, (F) hands-on activities, and (G) extracurricular opportunities. The unifying idea throughout all of these particulars is that the middle school curriculum needs a dynamic comprehensiveness that addresses the wide range of academic needs that middle school students have, combined with the vast range of academic, vocational, and career considerations that middle school students should become more aware of and more experienced with.

More variety than elementary school. Less variety than high school. More academically challenging than elementary school. Less academically complex than high school. More real-world connections and applications than elementary school. Less frequent and less direct real-world involvement than during high school.

Simply being more than elementary school in an academic approach or less than high school in the academic approach cannot provide adequate specifics, yet does give some qualitative description. The more-than-elementary-school and less-than-high-school guidelines do provide reminders that middle school is unique and is in the middle.

Middle school students should bring sufficient academic preparation and foundation for challenging, meaningful, and rewarding instructional experiences. Reality does show that some middle school students did not master the elementary school academic basics. What is to be done? Define today's reality and move in determined, daily steps toward the intended results.

No matter what academic achievements or lack of achievements are brought to middle school by entering 6th graders, the academic achievements of exiting 8th graders must be at or above grade level. Why? Because if academic success does not happen in middle school it is less likely to happen in high school.

Also, if middle school is merely a three-year holding pattern in which academically competent, advanced, or gifted students rarely experience a real challenge, these students can lose some of their enthusiasm for learning. If middle school experiences do challenge and do fascinate these accomplished students, their middle school results expand and they take with them to high school an accelerated academic success level and work ethic. They also develop a potentially lifelong learning ethic.

What is a learning ethic? One of the concepts of education in recent decades was "All students can learn, and at high levels." Some people may respond to that statement with "That is unrealistic," or "That is the goal," or "That is a dream, but education is a place for dreamers."

Are all students willing to learn? Are all students willing to learn at high levels? How is that willingness, if present, best applied? How is that willingness, if missing, somehow created, started, cultivated, developed? How is that willingness to learn, if only partially active, more thoroughly extended?

Middle school is a vital time to apply, nurture, extend, or start the learning ethic of students. If a willingness to learn does not exist in a 6th, 7th, or 8th grader, then delaying the effort to ignite and to begin that willingness to learn until "Oh, maybe something in high school will convince him to finally get interested in learning what school teaches" is asking for failure. One, two, or three years of middle school during which a student with zero or little learning ethic stays at the zero-to-little level means the habit of resisting learning becomes more ingrained.

For students who already have a good or superior learning ethic in middle school, these are the years to propel them into academic frontiers where new learning is vibrantly sought and experienced daily.

How is learning ethic begun in or developed in middle school students? Through a properly designed middle school curriculum implemented with effective instruction provided by teachers who thrive in the middle school setting, supported by counselors, administrators, and staff who devote themselves continuously to maximizing the middle school learning experience for students and the middle school work experience for teachers.

Let's consider three middle school students: their individual learning ethic and their experiences with the middle school curriculum, academics, and extracurricular activities.

Maria is a 6th grader who loves to learn. She reads a lot on her own. The school library is one of her favorite places, not just of the places at school, but everywhere. Maria was a good student in elementary school, but after one semester of middle school she has become an exemplary student. What changed, why did it change, and how did it change? Maria, Maria's mother, and Maria's language arts teacher each have an answer that reflects a unique perspective but which combines into a comprehensive perspective.

Maria's answer includes her sense of achievement:

> It was the contest. I came in second place. That was so cool. My prize was two books. I won two books and I got to pick them out from this really huge group of neat books.
>
> Here's how I got in the contest. My language arts teacher told us that we had to check out a book from the school library. Well, I can read OK, but I'd rather play soccer. I mean who would sit at home and read a book when you could go outside and play soccer? So, reading for me was what I did when I had to because there was some school homework or because the weather keeps me from playing soccer.
>
> So we go to the library to check out a book and I'm thinking, you know, it will be the usual books—school stuff, like really important people or really important things that happened.
>
> Then I see this book about soccer. It was written by a lady who played soccer in high school and then in college and even tried out for a World Cup team. It was so cool. So I checked out that book and read it as fast as I could.
>
> We had to write a paper about our book or make a poster or create a pamphlet. We had to show that we read the book and really understood it. So I wrote my paper like the book was a soccer game and I was the announcer for the game. My teacher loved my paper. She got this neat idea that I should film myself doing the announcing.
>
> Well, that was cool. So we put together this video with pictures of a soccer match, and with pictures of soccer fans, and with pictures of a soccer stadium. And all the time you hear me telling the story of this book.
>
> So the teacher told us that she was working with the school librarian on a contest. We had until the end of October to see who could read the most pages. We had to use library books and for each book we read we had to do a project to show that we really read the book.
>
> I went back to the library and we found another book about soccer, plus two books about television broadcasts of sports. This was September so I was playing in my fall soccer league and I was reading about soccer. School never had anything to do with soccer before. In October the contest ranking showed I was in fourth place. Well, I like to win so I checked out two more books.

One book was on Abraham Lincoln. I knew we would study him in history someday so I wanted to be ready. The other book was written by a person who knows a lot about money. My parents tell me that I have to start earning some of my own money. So, that book showed me how a twelve-year-old can do that.

By the end of October I had read six books, that was 1,057 pages. I had done all of that in about two months. I never read six books in a whole year. I came in second in the book reading contest. My prize was two books that I got to pick out from all of the books at a book fair our school had. The two books I picked out would have cost me about $30. I'm going to give one book to my brother and the other book to my sister for Christmas presents. That means I spend zero money on those presents. How's that for being smart with money?

One other thing. There's not a contest going on about reading now, but I'm still doing more reading. I never knew that the school library had so many books that I am interested in. I like computers and stuff like that, but my grandmother tells me that there is something better about holding onto a book. I think she's pretty old-fashioned, but, you know, books are better than I thought.

So the book contest really got me started. Now I'm reading on my own. Pretty neat, huh? Who knows? Maybe someday I'll write a book.

Maria's language arts teacher had not used this exact project before. Maria's class of twenty-seven students in first period 6th grade language arts was underachieving individually and collectively from the start of the school year. The teacher, Mrs. Sheffield, has eleven years of middle school teaching experience and she is a superior teacher. Yet Mrs. Sheffield realized after a few days with Maria's class that their reading skills, writing skills, and spelling skills were not at the 6th grade level.

Mrs. Sheffield faced a moment similar to moments that many teachers face. It was time to light a candle or to curse the darkness. Mrs. Sheffield could bemoan the factors that had caused this class of twenty-seven students to be unprepared for and to be disinterested in their language arts class. She had no interest in blaming the prior teachers of these students or in condemning the families or in criticizing the students themselves. Mrs. Sheffield chose to confidently and persistently deal with reality. Here's how she explains it.

I know the curriculum for language arts classes at the 6th, 7th, and 8th grade levels. The language arts teachers spend a lot of time every summer to update and fine-tune our language arts curriculum. We know exactly what skills must be mastered at each grade level. We don't send unprepared students to the 7th grade or on to the 8th grade. But we have no real control over what the 6th graders bring with them when they start middle school.

I have attended a few meetings with some elementary school teachers, but elementary schools and middle schools in this school district are in separate buildings that are usually far apart. So we really don't have much communication or interaction with elementary school teachers. I do have a copy of the language arts curriculum for kindergarten through 5th grade, but that just tells me what the students were supposed to learn.

During the first and second weeks of middle school, I give my 6th graders several tests to evaluate their spelling, reading, and writing accomplishments. Maria's class showed me from the start of the school year that they were not ready for 6th grade work. Unfortunately that happens some years, but it does not change what they have to learn during 6th grade. What changes is how I teach them because I have to get them up to 6th grade level quickly and I have to make sure they master all 6th grade content. It's not easy, but it can be done.

So, in the first week of school I had to make some creative adjustments. I assigned Maria's class the responsibility of each student writing a short autobiography. Students are experts about themselves and they usually like to tell people something about themselves. So I gave them some questions to answer such as, "Tell about a situation when you were very young and you learned a really important lesson." I also gave them a list of twenty vocabulary words and they had to use at least ten of those words in their autobiography. Spelling counted. Subjects and verbs had to match.

We evaluated some sample autobiographies I provided for them. I had written an autobiography as if it were for a person old enough to be the students' grandparent, another one as if it were for a person old enough to be their parent or guardian, and one more for a person who could be their older sister. In all of those samples I used the twenty vocabulary words on the list the students were given. Spelling was perfect. Subjects and verbs agreed exactly.

The students knew that they could not borrow sentences or ideas from the samples. They also knew that the samples showed that this assignment could be done. We did a little work in class on the autobiographies as each student wrote the opening paragraph of his or her autobiography. Plus, everyone outlined the rest of their papers. We did all of this on a Wednesday and the papers were due on Friday.

I made a big deal about the papers on Thursday. The principal helped. She had agreed to come read her autobiography to the class. The 6th grade guidance counselor also came to read his autobiography. Of course, some of the students asked me if I was going to read my autobiography. I was glad to do that. Then the students had read three samples and had heard three more sample autobiographies. I was eagerly awaiting Friday.

One student came up to me before class on Friday to say that he had not done the assignment. I had already seen his first paragraph and his outline that he did in class. I knew he had begun. I told him to sit down right now and finish it. He did. I wondered if he had been required to complete work in 5th grade, but that was not the issue. The issue was for him to get his work done. He finished it.

The results were good. Not perfect, but good. Every student turned in an autobiography.

Several of the papers were great. A few were less than I hoped for, but at least I had something to work with from every student. Plus, now I knew more about the students individually. That is what led to the book project and the reading contest.

I made a list of all the interests that students mentioned in their autobiographies. At the age of eleven or twelve, there were some students in this class who had learned about repairing cars, others know how to cook, several of them liked sports, some mentioned music including school or church groups they had performed with.

So I asked the librarian if the school library had enough books on all of these topics so each student had choices. I was told yes, there were lots of books about cars, sports, food, music, and every other topic the students had included in their autobiographies as important experiences or as something that interested them.

My experience with middle school students is that many of them like contests or competitions or keeping score in most anything. One math teacher at this school tries to make everything into a game or a contest. It's not always girls against boys or one group versus another, although that is done sometimes. It's usually each student competing against how he or she did in class the day before or the week before. That way the goal is not to be better than someone else, it's to be better than your own personal best results so far.

We're going to do that with the next reading contest. Each student will have to read more pages than they did in the first contest, but that's not all. There will be a prize for the first, second, and third students who get to 2,000 total pages for the year. So you can win by reading more than you did last time, but it is easier to go from 400 to 500 pages than from 1,000 to 1,100 pages. We also have some prizes when you get to 1,250 pages and 1,500 pages. I'm sure we will invent more improvements as we go through the year.

So the autobiography project worked. It led to the book reading contest. Every student in Maria's class read at least one book. During the two months of the contest students turned in, every week, a list of at least ten new vocabulary words they came across in the book they were reading. We put those twenty-seven lists on small posters each week. Students moved from list to list each Wednesday until they had read each list. Then we played a fast-paced vocabulary, definition, and spelling game. They loved it.

By November I was convinced that this class had caught up with where they needed to be in reading, writing, and spelling for 6th graders. My hope now is that they will surpass every 6th grade language arts requirement so they will be more than prepared for 7th grade.

Here's a big surprise. This 6th grade class asked me if our school could start a reading club. Then they asked if we could have a reading team that could somehow compete with reading teams from other middle schools. Well, we started the reading club and it is growing. Teachers, students, and parents or guardians read the same book. We sell snacks after school to raise the money to buy a copy of the book of the month for everyone who is involved. Our first month was such a success. We're excited. The students are excited. Reading is vital in our curriculum. Whoever thought that reading could become part of our extracurricular activities also?

Brad is a 7th grader who is fully capable of doing 8th grade work. He could probably do very well with 9th grade classes, but putting a twelve-year-old in the 9th grade raises some concerns. Yet having a very scholarly 7th grader who needs and seeks intellectual challenges endure an ordinary 7th grade year of academic content he already knows or will very easily master is not ideal. What is to be done?

There are other students at Brad's middle school who are quite capable of doing 9th grade work. If those students cannot yet go to high school, one creative approach could be to have high school come to them. Students in 6th, 7th, and 8th grade who can do 9th grade work could attend a class together at their middle school that is taught by a teacher at the middle school who is certified to teach 9th grade in particular or high school in general.

There are many valid reasons to organize middle school by grade levels; however, that structure does not have to control all options. Being a 7th grader chronologically does not mean that in all areas of academic work the student is exactly at 7th grade level. Much is done, as it should be, to get all students up to their grade level of academic achievement. Often, less is done, but that omission is unacceptable for high-achieving students whose demonstrated and measured academic accomplishment puts them above their current grade level.

Brad's school kept the existing grade level structure and teaching team structure that had been in place for many years, but two new classes were added: 9th grade geometry and 9th grade English. There were twenty-three geometry students from grades 7 and 8 in this new class, including Brad. There were twenty-four students, again including Brad, in the 9th grade English class. These classes began at the start of the school year when Brad was beginning 7th grade, but Brad felt like he was more than a 7th grader. He was in the middle school building, but he was also in the 9th grade curriculum.

Comments from students, teachers, the principal, and some parents showed how productive this approach was. Brad was very excited and said, "This is so cool. I'm taking 9th grade classes and I'm just in 7th grade. I really want to skip 8th grade and go straight to high school. I could graduate one year early. I could be in high school with my brother; he's a junior now. These classes are hard, but at least I'm learning. My other classes are just the same old stuff."

The geometry teacher was just as pleased. "These students are so motivated to learn. They work hard. They pay attention. They ask questions. They do the homework. I wonder if we've made middle school too easy or too simple overall. Maybe other middle school students could do this type of work if we just make it the plan for almost every student if we were sure they could succeed."

Brad's father was very supportive. "Brad made straight A's in 6th grade and almost never had any work to do. He knew everything they were doing. He had no reason to be excited about 7th or 8th grades. Now he is working harder than ever and he loves it. We are seriously considering asking that he be allowed to take 8th grade classes in the second semester of this year, finish the two 9th grade classes he has and move on to high school next year. He does not need to be in middle school for three years."

The middle school principal evaluated the 9th grade classes at the end of the first semester. The results were great. All but two students in geometry were doing well. In conversations with those two students and their families it was agreed that they would move to 8th grade math at the start of the second semester. A similar change was made in the 9th grade English class for one 7th grader and one 8th grader who would both move to 8th grade English for the second semester. The other twenty-one geometry students and twenty-two students in 9th grade English would continue those classes during the second semester.

The principal of the middle school had already talked to some high school counselors and administrators about how to place these advanced students in high school when they finished middle school. The tentative plan was that students who made an A or B grade in geometry or 9th grade English would be placed in the next class in the math or English sequence, but no credit toward high school graduation would be given for the high school level classes taken this year.

That would change. If high school seniors could take dual credit classes that count as a high school credit toward graduation and that also count as a college two- or three-hour course, then there was a precedent. All of the proper procedures were followed so in the next year "early high school" classes taught at the middle school could potentially earn actual credit toward high school graduation. The student must make an A or B grade in each semester and must score at the 85th percentile or above on a nationally normed standardized test in geometry or 9th grade English.

The two teachers involved with teaching the geometry and 9th grade English classes made it very clear that they would like to continue this work in upcoming years. Other teachers suggested expanding the plan to include other equivalent classes in science or social studies. The potential for middle school students to complete part of 9th grade while still in middle school was appealing to a growing number of students and their families. This plan was not ideal for everyone, but it was one more way to guide one more group of students through the middle school maze. For these students the worst part of that maze was the repetition and the lack of challenge. For those students, middle school academics presented very little that was new or was demanding. That was changing with the early high school concept.

Tyler barely passed 7th grade. He barely passed 6th grade. In fact, he had to go to summer school to make up two classes after his 6th grade year and he had to go summer school after 7th grade to make up two classes he failed that year.

Tyler enters 8th grade with a 5th grade reading level, with very limited math skills, and with an attitude about school that says he cannot wait to drop out as soon as he is old enough to do that legally.

Tyler misbehaves at school intentionally. He tries to get suspended. Being suspended from school is the closest option he has to dropping out. He fails classes on purpose and then does three weeks of minimal work on a computerized tutorial program in the summer to make up classes. He does not care about making up the classes, but he likes computers and if he goes to summer school he is given breakfast and lunch, so he does all of this intentionally.

Tyler's 8th grade math teacher was stunned by Tyler's defiance and vulgarity in class on the first day of school. He called the office immediately for an administrator to deal with Tyler. The assistant principal knew Tyler from the past two years. He intended to outsmart Tyler.

The assistant principal arrived at the math classroom accompanied by the school's social worker. Tyler left the class and went with these two adults to the school's gym, which was not used during this class period. The assistant principal and the social worker had created their plan earlier. Tyler was to shoot two hundred free throws and then he would do many mathematical calculations based on the results of his free-throw shooting. He would then do the same calculations after he took fifty three-point shots. Tyler obeyed and he never used vulgar language during class again.

What Tyler did not know was that his math class of twenty-two students was made up completely of students who are two years or more behind grade level in reading and who are at a low percentile on math standardized tests. This class is 8th grade math, but there is no textbook and there are no generic worksheets.

There are basketball statistics, football statistics, baseball statistics, money calculations, food comparisons for calories or costs, job analysis for income and qualifications, analysis of public opinion polls, conducting public opinion polls at school, budgeting, car calculations of purchase cost or repair, and guest speakers. The guests would range from business owners to the local jailer, from police officers to directors of charities, from health care providers to drug law enforcement officials.

The class was designed to be a form of practical, everyday math applications combined with practical, everyday realities. The students in the class need to learn math lessons and need to learn practical life skills lessons. Each of the students will be monitored closely by the school's social worker.

Some people saw the class as a dropout prevention program. Other people saw it as a crime prevention program. The middle school principal, counselors, social worker, and teachers saw the class as dealing with reality. The students in the class are far behind academically, get in trouble often, have been court involved or seem to be headed in that direction, and cause continuous problems at school. Something different had to be done.

Tyler hit 138 out of the 200 free throws. He made 18 out of 50 three-point shots. He got some of the basketball math problems right as he calculated his shooting percentages and then contrasted himself with high school, college, and professional basketball statistics.

Tyler said to the social worker, "Hey, I'm as good as they are. I'm better than some college players. That's crazy. I'm even better than some pro players. How does that make sense?"

The social worker realized a teaching moment. "Tyler, your shooting statistics are good, so why aren't sports reporters writing stories about you?"

No answer for a few moments, then this reply, "Because they're stupid. They don't care about me. They just do easy stuff. They write about famous people."

The social worker agreed. "That's true. So let's make you famous."

Tyler was confused. "How can I ever be famous?"

That was easy to answer. "Tyler, it's like this. You have to learn to read better. You can't get suspended any more. You have to obey teachers and you must follow rules. You have to work. Then you have to earn the grades that make you eligible for the basketball team tryouts. Plus, you have to do something for other people. There are school service activities like helping to collect recycled materials here. Do things like that to show you care about this place.

"Then when your grades are up, your behavior is up, and you have better basketball statistics than college or pro players, I can tell a local news reporter. You just might be famous."

Tyler liked the idea. "You'd do that for me? Really? You'd, like, tell a news reporter and stuff? They might write a story about me?"

The social worker was very sincere. "Let's find out, Tyler. You do the work that gives me a story to tell the reporter and I'll tell them. They aren't going to write about you nearly failing 6th and 7th grade or you getting kicked out of 8th grade math class on the first day of school. Give them something really good, really amazing to write. It's really up to you."

The school did not just put Tyler in a typical math class that he would probably fail and that he would likely misbehave in. This middle school took decisive action to combine curriculum, academics, and extracurricular activities into a motivating experience that says to Tyler, "We are doing our part, now you team up with us and everyone wins." With opportunities like that being made available to students by middle school educators and staff, mastering the middle school maze becomes a journey that students realize is worth serious effort.

The middle school maze has some obstacles, challenges, difficulties, and problems that most or almost all middle school students will encounter. The middle school maze has unique twists and turns, hills and barriers that have an individualized uniqueness with each student. The result is that some of the middle school curriculum, academic programs, and extracurricular activities can usefully serve the majority of students. Other students need the academics, the curriculum, and the extracurricular options to creatively adapt in ways that address what is best for Maria, Brad, Tyler, and each student in the school.

When the overall curriculum, academic program, and extracurricular activities do provide what is needed for most students, some of those students—at various times, each of those students—could need a creative variation on the curriculum, academic program, or extracurricular activities.

A precisely planned and scripted three-year academic program that says to a 6th grader, "Follow this plan for the next 540 school days, never stray from this plan, and on day 541 you will be permitted to conclude middle school and register for high school" is a plan that works better for machines rather than for people. Machines repeatedly perform the same task. Middle school students benefit from structure yet thrive when creativity, innovation, and individuality are included.

Machines are used when the goal is for each product to be identical. No mechanistic, bureaucratic, programmed package of educational edicts and procedures imposed on a middle school will transform the individual journeys through the middle school maze into a lock-step three-year training program that conforms each middle school student into a regimented trainee.

One scientific law states that a body in motion stays in motion until acted upon by an outside force. Mr. Newton's scientific revelation is a reminder that middle school students are people, minds, emotions, ideas, questions, and bodies that are in a type of perpetual motion. There are pauses in some of those motions, but few complete stops. The middle school student who sits somewhat still at a desk for one hour in a classroom could still be quite vibrant in thought, in emotion, in questions, and in distractions.

The middle school academic program content cannot vary daily. The established curriculum must be implemented, yet how that is done can vary daily. To do otherwise is to falsely assume that the best way for a 6th grader to learn in September is also the best way for that 6th grader to learn in April and, for that matter, is forever the best way for every 6th grader to learn always.

One creative blend of academics and extracurriculars is an activity period held perhaps monthly during the school day. Teachers and staff members are asked what activities they could sponsor. The topics of faculty and staff interest or expertise could range from sewing to cake decorating, from comic books to drama, from computers to politics, from gardening to creative writing, from sports to fashion.

Students are then given the list of activity topics that teachers have said they could sponsor. The students list their first, second, third, and fourth choices. Then the roster is made for each activity period group. Making these rosters is very time consuming, so be prepared. Perhaps the sign-up and roster lists could be done electronically to simplify the process. Even if pencil, paper, and hours are involved, the results are worth the investment of much time.

Activity period rosters are posted throughout the school. Each teaching team gets a copy so they can tell every student on their team which activity they are involved with, who the sponsor is, and where they will meet. The school schedule could be adjusted to take five to ten minutes from each class to create time for activity period. It may work to just substitute activity period for a class period on a rotating basis so no class period is missed more than twice in a school year. The ideal schedule will vary from school to school.

It is 2:15 at a middle school that will have activity period from 2:20 until 3:20. The excitement is growing and the anticipation builds. An announcement is made to explain, one more time, what everyone will do when the next bell rings. After the announcement each teacher confirms with each of his or her students that everyone knows which activity they report to and where that group will meet. The bell rings to end class and now everyone moves to their activity period group.

The teachers and staff members check attendance. The administrators check the halls and bathrooms for students who are genuinely unsure where to go and for students who planned to skip activity period. The administrators then visit many of the activity groups. The cooking club is making pizza. The baseball card group members are considering trades. The chess group is intensely thinking about moves and counter-moves. The dance group appears to be Broadway-bound. Everyone is in an activity and everyone is active.

One teaching team evaluated activity period the next day. The consensus was that students loved the activities. The other major evaluation points were that (1) teacher/staff and student interaction was so very cordial, sincere, and meaningful and (2) there must be some way to get the excitement and involvement levels of activity period to occur in the classroom regularly.

This teaching team decided to create a day of class activities that applied the topics and tasks of activity period. Math and cooking were a good match. There are so many numbers that relate to food that any middle school math skill could somehow connect with food and cooking.

The English teacher was confident that grammar and comic books could connect. She envisioned a super-hero team to rescue words that were misspelled or misused. Captain Comma, General Gerund, Corporal Conjunction, Sargent Subject, Verb Man, and Word Woman would soon be good friends of the students.

Activity period was once per month. Application of activity period endeavors became fairly common in classrooms regularly. One idea—activity period—can have a big impact on a middle school as the curriculum, the academic program, and the extracurricular opportunities merge into a best-of-all-worlds approach.

Hard work? Yes. Great results? Quite possible. Worth a try? Yes. One more way to help middle school students navigate the middle school maze? Yes, along with many other ideas that each middle school can create or borrow depending on what they need to achieve and on what works best for the unique students, environment, and educators at a given school, at each unique middle school.

In the next chapter full emphasis will be on a topic that has punctuated the prior chapters: why it is so important to get everything right in middle school.

To closely connect chapters 8 and 9, we will meet Travis, an 8th grader. His experiences during and his thoughts about a day of middle school classes show that as the curriculum, academic program, and extracurricular activities are designed and implemented well, the results can be that middle school years are done right and those years establish a firm foundation for high school success.

"This bus is so crowded. There's never enough room. My friend says his bus has lots of room. We need another bus."

Travis Mitchell was right. His school days always began with a fifteen-minute ride on a very crowded bus. The only benefit was that when the bus arrived at Northwood Middle School all of the students on the bus were eager to get off the bus and into the school.

Travis always eats breakfast at home, but a lot of students at Northwood did go to the school cafeteria for breakfast. Travis spent the early morning time at school in the library. Computers were available for students to use. Travis had learned in 6th grade that it was really easy to keep up with homework if you used the thirty or so minutes between arriving at school and going to first period class. Travis used this time to finish anything that was due soon or to get ahead of a project that would be due soon.

The other benefit of going to the library right after getting to school was that you avoided the cafeteria and the gym. Those were the only other places students could be until it was time to go to their lockers and then to first period class.

Travis usually arrived at school about 8:00 a.m. and he stayed in the library until 8:27 a.m., when the bell rang to send everyone to lockers and to first period class. Students were to be in their desk in their class by the time the 8:35 a.m. bell rang. There was a warning bell at 8:33 a.m.

Travis was always on time to his classes. The school was serious about punctuality. Being late to class three times meant you had to stay after school. Travis had better things to do when the school day ended, so he made sure he was on time, always.

First period math class was not Travis's favorite.

We do the same stuff every day. The teacher puts five problems on the board. We do one more problem that a student puts on the board. I hate it when I have to put the problem on the board. No matter what I do the teacher finds something wrong. Then we get a worksheet with ten problems to do. Then we get our homework assignment, which usually is the odd-numbered problems on some page in the book. We turn in the homework the next day and it all starts again.

Eighth grade math is the same as 7th grade math, which was not much different than 6th grade math. It's all pretty dumb if you ask me. My brother is in high school. He says their math classes are really cool. They do neat stuff like design a house and do all the math that goes into making a house. That sounds better than what we do. I know I have to do what the teacher tells me to. I just wish it was more interesting and, you know, I wish we didn't do the same thing every day.

My brother wants to have his own house construction company someday. He's in this neat program that lets him build a small building, a garage I think. Then they take it all apart. That would be so neat. I want to do something like that, but 8th graders don't get to.

Travis has science class during second period. He does not like science, but he does the work and always makes a good grade. It's easy because all they do is read the science book and take notes. Maybe once a month they do some experiment or laboratory project. "Those are so cool. I love the experiments. Science is neat when you actually get to see it happen and stuff. I think we ought to do a lot more experiments."

The school day gets a lot better for Travis during third period and fourth period. That's when Travis takes a new class called American studies. It's a combination of U.S. history, U.S. government, and American literature. Travis has the same teacher for the two class periods that add up to the American studies class.

Some days they do a lot of U.S. history and not so much U.S. government or American literature. Other days they could do a lot of U.S. government or a lot of American literature. No two days are exactly alike. They do skits. The use computers, they write stories, they use videos, they take virtual tours of museums or of historical landmarks. The classroom looks like a museum with historical items, student work on display, and lots of books.

Travis got to do a project on the history of American architecture. He had no idea how people in the colonies built homes. He knew nothing about how skyscrapers were built in the late 1800s. Now, Travis knows all about these topics, plus he found out how to do the research that showed him all about colonial homes and about 1890 skyscrapers. Because of that research experience Travis now knows how to find out details about any topic.

Lunch is at the end of fourth period class. "Lunch is great. I see my friends. I usually bring my lunch, but when the cafeteria has stuff I really like I go through the cafeteria line. Sometimes they have a salad bar or a baked potato bar. Those are the best. Lunch is cool because since middle school doesn't have recess, lunch is the only time we have to goof off."

Fifth period class finds Travis in an elective class. These classes are designed to let middle school students explore various topics for one-fourth of the school year. During fifth period this year Travis will have arts and humanities, Latin, computer applications, and physical education.

Travis has a second elective class during sixth period. This band class meets all year, but Travis is going to quit the band because he is not going to be in band in high school and he would rather try some new electives later this year. So in the second semester he will take Career Planning and then Money Management. Those electives sound great to Travis because he intends on a successful career and on some degree of financial success.

The school day concludes for Travis with seventh period class. This class is the same for all 6th, 7th, and 8th graders at Travis' school. The study skills class combines study hall with individual instruction. The teacher makes sure that each student has written the homework assignments for the next day. The Web pages of all teachers on the teaching team are viewed on the screen in the classroom. The teacher checks every student's planner to be sure the assignments are written down accurately. Then students begin doing their homework under the structured supervision of the teacher.

No electronic gadgets are allowed. No socializing is tolerated. Schoolwork must be done. Once a week the teacher provides instruction on topics such as time management, reading skills, note-taking for all classes, research skills, school rules, and, for 8th graders, what to expect in high school.

Once each week Travis participates after school in the Car Repair Club. The principal arranged with the owner of a local car repair shop to work with a group of ten 8th graders who earned the opportunity to join this club.

Requirements were (1) no discipline incidents that had resulted in suspension from school, (2) no unexcused absences from school, (3) no F grades in any class, and (4) complete a written application and an in-person interview.

The school's technology director also helps sponsor this club. The combination of hands-on work to actually repair a car and sophisticated technological analysis of how computers work in cars has fascinated Travis. He can see himself doing this type of work although he also likes the idea of building houses with his brother. Both options interest Travis and motivate Travis. Northwood Middle School has helped Travis establish goals and plans along with beginning to master the skills that can make those goals and plans actually happen.

Travis does need a better experience in his math and science classes. He will get better elective options in the second semester so the school is working with Travis and his family to make the school schedule work better for Travis. The study skills class helped Travis get into good time management habits and good study habits during middle school. The middle school librarian has communicated with the high school librarian to be sure that Travis can use the high school library some mornings before school starts. The middle school technology director has contacted a middle school counselor and a high school counselor to be sure that Travis has more opportunities to take classes that build on his skills in and interests in construction and in car repair.

Travis will have many good results to show for his middle school years. He will take a solid foundation for further achievement with him to high school. Without the very favorable impact of early morning library time, a fascinating American studies program, the varied elective class offerings, the highly structured study skills program, and the car repair experience, Travis might have just wandered through middle school with a good-enough-to-get-by record. Instead, Travis has been given three middle school years of meaningful accomplishments. Travis's middle school got middle school to work well for him. Travis also worked well. The symbiosis is superior.

Northwood Middle School got middle school right—not perfect, but right for Travis. Science and math instruction at the 8th grade level need to improve. Other factors were favorable. Travis's middle school years have been productive, important, and impactful. The middle school experience was right for Travis because many people worked to make it right.

What happens if the middle school experience is not right? What happens if Travis leaves middle school without new skills, new abilities, new knowledge, or a direction for achievement in high school? What happens if Travis leaves middle school very similar to how he entered middle school? If middle school works right for Travis, what possibilities then await him in high school? If middle school does not work right for Travis, what possibilities do not await him in high school? Thoughts such as those will be explored in the next chapter.

Chapter Nine

Why It Is So Important to Get Everything Right in Middle School

Habits. Skills. Work ethic. Learning ethic. Manners. Intellectual curiosity. Habits. Intellectual activity. Discipline. Time management. Obedience. Responsibility. Cooperation. Habits.

Students who bring proper work habits and behavior habits with them from elementary school to middle school will benefit further from middle school experiences that apply, develop, and improve those good work habits and those good behavior habits. Middle school can guide these students from good habits to superior habits.

Students who bring ordinary, average, fair, or barely acceptable work habits and behavior habits into middle school need direct interventions immediately and continuously. The ordinary work habits or behavior habits of an eleven-year-old 6th grader could become permanent if they are unchanged when that student finishes 8th grade.

For students who bring bad work habits or no work habits and no work ethic with them into 6th grade, the tasks facing the middle school educators are immensely difficult and are quite urgent. Thorough analysis, evaluation, and intervention will be needed. Blunt questions such as, "Can this student read?" must be asked directly and answered honestly. A barely literate or actually illiterate 6th grader needs for literacy to be the magnificent obsession of his or her education until grade-level literacy is attained.

Sixth graders whose misbehavior habits include defiance, disrupting class, bullying, stealing, drug use (including alcohol), skipping classes, vulgar language, ignoring instructions, cheating, refusing to work, fighting, or vandalism or other violations of laws, policies, or rules, need immediate and direct intervention as soon as any of these problems surface in middle school. Specialized programs or intense interventions at the middle school may be needed. Alternative educational programs may merit consideration and use.

The eleven-, twelve-, or thirteen-year-old 6th graders whose academics and/or behavior results in elementary school confirm that the student is not at all prepared for middle school is at risk of failure academically and is at risk for disruptive, damaging, or illegal misbehaviors. The most serious and intense interventions or alternatives may be needed or this student will be ingrained with the habits of academic failure, behavior failure, court involvement, and underachievement.

Some 6th graders begin middle school with academic achievements and skills that show their school performance is already far beyond 6th grade. Some 6th graders begin middle school with maturity, manners, integrity, personal discipline, and people skills that are beyond their years. It is unacceptable to assume that these students who are exemplary in academics and in ethics "will do fine." They need academic challenges to exercise, to apply, to build, to extend their knowledge. They need interactive opportunities to apply and to strengthen their honorable people skills. Arriving at middle school above grade level in academics and/or in behavior does not guarantee that the student will conclude the middle school three years later similarly or even more above grade level in academics and above age level in character, ethics, manners, or people skills.

Bad habits that remain bad during the middle school years can become ingrained or nearly ingrained, whether it be academics or behavior. Good habits that are not applied, acknowledged, nurtured, developed, and extended during the middle school years can decline, reverse, or atrophy. What is not corrected or developed in middle school is less likely to be corrected or developed in high school.

Why? Among the reasons are these two: (1) The habits of a fourteen-year-old 9th grader have had three years to become more firmly entrenched than the habits of an eleven-year-old 6th grader. Add three years of repeated bad habits and changing those habits has become much more difficult and much less likely. (2) Middle schools are usually smaller in enrollment than are high schools and the use of teaching teams in middle schools further personalize the awareness that teachers have of each individual student. These are among the factors that indicate why it is so important to get everything right in middle school.

Reality is that there will be less likelihood in high school of correcting what is still wrong. High schools can help students make drastic corrections, but the age group involved with high school, the other demands on or distractions impacting student time, work, and attention, and the solidified habits formed and kept by the start of high school all make high school turnarounds, while still possible, increasingly difficult. The following case studies personalize the importance of getting middle school right.

ELLEN—FROM 6TH GRADE SUCCESS TO 8TH GRADE SUPER SUCCESS

Ellen Fletcher could not wait for the first day of middle school. Her older sister, Angela, had told her all about the teachers, the classes, the clubs, the sports, the rules, the schedule, and who she really needed to meet. Ellen's sister had just finished middle school so Angela was quite an expert; at least Ellen thought she was.

Ellen had won several awards at the end of 5th grade. She won the librarian's award for having read more books than any other 5th grader. Those twenty-eight books were read, were written about, and were tested on. Ellen read every word in each of the books. She intended to meet the middle school librarian soon and get started on reading as many books as possible during her years in middle school.

Ellen also won an award at the 5th grade science fair. Her project was about use of electronic reading devices versus reading traditional books. She won first place in the technology category of the science fair.

Ellen won two other awards at the end of 5th grade. She was named the school's most exemplary citizen. This was due to canned food drives that Ellen organized at Thanksgiving and at Christmas. Another reason Ellen won this award was because she had perfect attendance in 3rd, 4th, and 5th grades. She also had zero discipline incidents or demerits during her elementary school years and she won an award for this.

Ellen did have two concerns about middle school. First, the building is really big and it might be easy to get lost. It would be so embarrassing to get lost or to walk into the wrong room or to be late for class. Angela and Ellen visited the school twice before the first day of school, but Ellen still wondered what would happen when seven hundred or eight hundred students filled the place and she had to find her way through that crowd.

Ellen also was wondering how she would do in math class. Ellen was great in reading and in science, but math was always a struggle for her. She got her math work done and she paid extra close attention to everything teachers taught about math, but math just never came easy to Ellen in elementary school. She was actually a bit anxious and uncertain about how she would do with middle school math. Angela showed her something about algebra and Ellen thought that was very confusing. Still, she was generally confident and excited on the first day of middle school.

Ellen's middle school did things differently for 6th graders on the first day of school. The regular schedule takes students to eight classes during the day, but on the first day of school, 6th graders stay with their first period teacher for the first half of the day of school. The morning of the first day of middle school was very busy for every 6th grader.

Rules. The first thing the teacher talked about was rules. School rules. Sixth grade rules. Rules about the cafeteria and the library, the hallways and the computer lab, the gymnasium and the school buses. There were so many rules. There was a video to watch about school bus safety. There was a video to watch that had the principal and the assistant principal welcoming everyone and explaining rules. There was a quiz to take about rules.

Then Ellen's class got their lockers. The challenge was to get the combination of the lock to work. The lock was built into the locker so a lock did not have to be purchased. Three turns to the right, hit the number, two turns to the left, hit the number, back to the right and stop at the last number. It just would not work. Ellen wondered why her locker did not open while other lockers opened easily. The teacher showed Ellen how it is done. It is important to hit the numbers exactly and when Ellen did that it worked fine.

Then Ellen's group took a tour of the school. This was the best part of the morning because when they arrived at the library they stayed for a long time. The librarian showed them how to find any particular book and explained how to check out a book. Ellen asked if there were any reading contests or things like that. She was thrilled to find out that there was a reading contest each month, a reading club, and visits from authors several times during the year. All of that was great news for Ellen.

Finally, it was time for lunch and that was really confusing. There were so many students in the cafeteria and there was not much time. The assistant principal kept everyone moving from place to place so everyone had a table to sit at, got to the serving line, and wasted no time. When lunch was over, Ellen and her group returned to the classroom where they had been all morning. There was one more discussion about rules so everyone understood how the rest of the day would go including the procedures for dismissal at the end of the day.

Ellen now went to math class. This was the one class she had real doubts about, but the teacher must have known that Ellen was concerned because as soon as Ellen walked into the classroom the teacher began talking to Ellen and to every student as they walked in. The teacher handed every student a two- or three-digit number that had been written on an index card. Nobody knew what the cards were for, but they looked fairly interesting.

The teacher called roll and instead of raising a hand or saying "here," each student said their number. If your index card had 73 written on it, you said, "Seventy-three." Then the teacher organized all of the students into pairs. Each pair of students took their two numbers and added them together, subtracted the smaller from the larger, and then multiplied them together. Each pair reported their results and the teacher checked the math as the reports were made.

Then the teacher put the students in groups of five and had them add their five numbers together. Each group reported their results. So far, 6th grade math made sense to Ellen. Then she was given her homework that was due the next day. The assignment was to go home and make a list of twenty ways that math was used in your home. An example was the numbers on a clock. Ellen was sure she could find twenty uses of numbers at her home. She quickly thought of the channels on the television, the temperature setting on the oven, and the street address of her house. Maybe 6th grade math would not be so bad.

The rest of the day was when Ellen had 6th period social studies class and then her two elective classes. During this quarter of the school year her electives were computer applications and Spanish. By the end of the day Ellen was ready to go home because it was a long school day, longer by twenty minutes than her elementary school day had been. Ellen walked home with two of her best 6th grade friends. They talked about everything that was different in middle school. It was a short walk to their neighborhood and the only busy intersection was supervised by a crossing guard, so all of the safety rules were enforced.

The high school dismissed before the middle school so Angela was already home. She had lots to tell Ellen about 9th grade and she had questions for Ellen. After they talked and had a snack, Ellen started working on her list for math class. There were uses of numbers all around the house, even on the tag their dog wore on his collar. Ellen decided to make a list of twenty-five uses of numbers at her home. Maybe the extra five items on her list would impress the teacher. When she finished making this list, she had some chores to do as part of her responsibilities to her family. Then she had some time to play outside. She had seen a sign at school about tryouts for the volleyball team and that interested her, so she called a friend who is in 7th grade and who played volleyball for the school last year. They decided to practice volleyball in Ellen's backyard.

Ellen's parents were eager to hear all about the first day of school. Ellen and Angela had lots to tell about. When Ellen's father asked her about math class she proudly showed him the homework she had completed including the extra work she did. He told her that she was probably the only person to do extra work and that she should keep doing extra math whenever she could.

Ellen's mother asked about the library and Ellen gave a detailed account. Angela encouraged Ellen to find out about being a student assistant in the library. A few students were chosen to help in the library during the time before class began each morning. This meant you got to go to the library each morning and you got to see the new books before anyone else did. Ellen would be sure to ask about that tomorrow.

Angela mentioned that all of her classes looked good. She said the high school was huge, two or three times larger than the middle school, but she found all of her classes and did not get lost. She said each teacher gave them a schedule of assignments for the first month of school. There was a lot of reading to do in every class, but that would be no real problem because reading had been the number one emphasis in middle school. Angela thought she was ready for high school and she really liked the variety of classes she could take in the next four years.

So, the first day of school went well for Ellen and for Angela. Angela's solid foundation of reading in middle school would be quite an asset for her in high school. Would Ellen's middle school experience be productive and meaningful so that the middle school years were maximized and so that she would be fully prepared for high school? The answer is found when we visit Ellen during her 8th grade year of middle school.

Ellen's 8th grade math teacher talked to her in October about becoming part of a group of 8th graders who tutor 6th graders in math. On Tuesday, some 6th graders come to a math classroom before first period class for math tutoring. Eighth graders who excel in math and who have excellent people skills are given the opportunity to help these 6th graders who need extra one-on-one guidance in math in addition to the instruction they get in class. Ellen really liked this idea. She checked with the librarian to be sure it would be acceptable to miss one day each week of her library work and the librarian was fine with that. So Ellen, who once had been apprehensive about middle school math, now was a middle school math tutor. What changed?

It all goes back to Ellen's experience in 6th grade math. The emphasis in the class was to completely master every part of the 6th grade math curriculum. The next emphasis was to become introduced to the basics of the 7th grade math curriculum. The third emphasis was to make math practical. The math teachers at Ellen's middle school were concerned that students perceived math as ordinary and repetitive problems to do from pages in a textbook or from worksheets. The teachers at Ellen's middle school worked together to create math activities and math lessons that enabled the students to learn math through very practical applications of math.

Ellen did participate in volleyball throughout her three years of middle school. The volleyball coaches worked with the math teachers to provide many volleyball statistics. This was also done by the coaches of every other sport, plus the sponsors of clubs. So the students found themselves analyzing sports statistics, environmental data, computer information, school fund-raising results, even school attendance data. Every math skill, function, and topic that middle school students had to learn could be connected with real-life, practical, interesting, and immediately applicable aspects of activities that 6th, 7th, and 8th graders cared about, were interested in, and were involved with.

Until middle school, Ellen had never seen that math mattered. In elementary school, math was something Ellen had to do because it was assigned. In middle school, math was something Ellen eagerly did because it mattered to her. It really made her a better volleyball player when she understood the statistics of a volleyball match. She was amazed that there was always a statistical explanation of why her team won or why her team lost. It was not just how many points were scored, but it went much deeper than that. The statistics, the math, always explained how and why points were scored or were not scored.

In 6th grade and in 7th grade, Ellen's volleyball team competed in the championship game among a group of twelve middle schools. They lost the championship when she was in 6th grade, but they came back the next year and won the league championship when Ellen was in 7th grade. Ellen is convinced that some extra volleyball statistical analysis helped her team in the 7th grade move from runner-up the previous year to champion in her 7th grade year. Math mattered in a way that truly inspired and fascinated Ellen. Because math mattered to Ellen and to other middle school students as they experienced the immediate benefit of math, the students and the teachers had very productive and meaningful math classes.

Ellen's work in the library made her feel as if she was needed by the school. The librarian realized how interested Ellen was in books, so whenever an author came to the school for a "book talk," Ellen was given the opportunity to meet the author, to ask questions, and to get a signed copy of the author's newest book. This experience in the library encouraged Ellen to follow the words on a banner in the library: "Read. Read More. Keep Reading."

Being an eager reader, an encouraged reader, gave Ellen an advantage in every class she took in middle school. English and social studies classes involved large amounts of reading. Science included reading and included much math calculation. The science teachers followed the example of the math teachers to make science practical and applicable. When 7th grade students analyzed the scientific aspects of cooking pizza, baking cookies, or consuming water versus soft drinks, the importance of knowing science increased greatly.

Ellen did some extra research on the benefits of drinking water. She shared that with her volleyball coach and with the volleyball team. The team members decided to not drink soft drinks during the volleyball season, but to drink water or sports beverages. Ellen was convinced that the team's improved results during her 7th grade year were supported by this nutritional advantage. She never would have expected that math and science could have anything to do with winning a volleyball championship, but she was convinced of that now.

Ellen's elective teachers made a lot of changes in their classes to avoid repetition. Eighth grade physical education classes needed to be more challenging and complex than 7th grade physical education class was. Seventh grade arts and humanities class needed to be more challenging and complex than 6th grade arts and humanities class had been. These teachers updated the curriculum so each subject had a more precise three-year sequence that built upon skills mastered and knowledge obtained in the prior year. Written tests and performance tests were given to confirm that knowledge and skills were mastered. If test results were below mastery for any student in any elective class, the student had to complete an individualized knowledge builder or skill builder activity to attain mastery.

By the end of the 8th grade, Ellen was reading at the eleventh grade level. She had been on the academic Honor Roll every grading period during middle school. She had mastered math, including algebra, and would take geometry as a 9th grader. She won an 8th grade science fair award for her detailed study of nutrition for athletes. She was named school volunteer of the year as an 8th grader for her work in the library and her work as a math tutor.

The middle school experience had been very good for Ellen. Her classes and the additional activities were designed for a middle school student to learn meaningfully right now. Middle school teachers had prepared Ellen well for high school, but that was not their highest goal. Ellen's teachers sought to maximize the results of middle school classes and activities for the immediate, right-now benefit, importance, and application.

Ellen's teachers knew that there was very little motivation in the statement, "Work hard now because you'll need this when you get to high school." Sure, middle school students anticipate high school and may eagerly await high school, but the real attention of middle school students is to "right here, right now."

Maximizing the results of middle school right here, right now, with and for middle school students provides the double benefit of increased achievements now and the foundation for increased achievements later. The next student we meet had a different middle school experience, for a variety of reasons, than Ellen Fletcher did.

MARTHA—THREE YEARS OF MIDDLE SCHOOL AND VERY FEW RESULTS, UNTIL . . .

Martha Anderson is in the 6th grade and is making very low grades. She made low grades in elementary school. Martha lives with her mother, her older brother, and her younger sister. Her mother is an emergency room nurse. Her brother is sixteen years old, is passing his high school classes, will graduate from high school on schedule, and has a part-time job at a fast food restaurant. Martha's younger sister is in the 4th grade at an elementary school that is separated by a playground from Martha's neighboring middle school. Martha and her younger sister ride the same bus to school each morning and then ride a bus home together in the afternoon.

Martha's teachers keep her mother updated about her grades and about her behavior. The teachers on Martha's teaching team have met with Martha's mother. The major problem is that Martha rarely does her homework, so her homework grades are low. Martha passes most of her tests, but with passing grades on tests and generally failing grades on homework, Martha is passing four classes and she is failing four classes. She is at risk to fail 6th grade.

Martha reads at the 6th grade level, but she does not complete all reading assignments. When students are given material to read in class, Martha makes a minimal effort to read it. She sometimes just blankly stares at the pages. Her teachers instruct her to read and she may make some limited effort right after a personal, direct instruction; however, that effort is inadequate to complete the assignment and to comprehend the assignment.

Martha has never failed a grade in school. She did have to attend a two-week catch-up program after 4th grade. This was for half days at her elementary school. The time was split between reading instruction, math instruction, study skills, and computer applications. The program was for 4th graders who passed 4th grade, but who needed some additional preparation for 5th grade. Breakfast and lunch were served, Martha got to see some friends, the school building was air conditioned, and transportation was provided, so Martha did not mind going.

In fact, Martha started wondering why should she work hard in school all year if she could make up what she missed with two easy weeks in the summer. The catch-up program lost its funding so Martha could not attend that two-week activity after 5th grade, but she had passed 5th grade so she did not give catching up any thought.

Martha passed 6th grade. She made D or C grades in all of her classes. She was interested in basketball, but she did not have the grades to be eligible to try out. Students were required to have a C average and Martha's grades were more D's than C's, so she could not try out. That bothered her a little because her athletic skills surpassed most of the students who made the team, but she decided that it was not so important to play basketball when there were other things to do.

What were those other things? Martha made some new friends during 7th grade. These students were new to Martha's middle school and she had some classes with them. One day at lunch these new friends told Martha they knew how to make a lot of money really easily. They needed Martha to steal stuff at school, then they would sell it and share the money with her. Martha's behavior at school was not perfect, but she never did anything serious like stealing. She knew it was wrong, but these new students said they never got in trouble when they did this at their old school, so Martha said she would try it once.

The plan was for Martha to get in the lockers of other students during physical education class. Martha would ask the teacher to let her go into the locker room to use the bathroom during class. She would steal a cell phone or other electronic devices or money while she was in the locker room. If people blamed her, she would blame other people who were just trying to get her in trouble. Martha even found a place to hide what she stole so it could not be found on her. She would get the stuff later and give it to her new friends who would sell it.

The plan fell apart. Martha stole one cell phone from a student and twenty dollars in cash from another student. Those students realized that their possessions were missing before they left physical education class. The teacher had everyone look throughout the locker room and the stolen items were found under equipment where Martha had put it. All of the evidence pointed toward Martha. Martha denied doing anything, but the evidence was too strong.

Should Martha blame her new friends because they put her up to stealing? She began to realize how much of a mistake she had made when she listened to her new friends. She realized that they were not friends; rather, they were just using her. The locker room scheme was a big mistake. Martha knew that stealing was wrong and she was the person who made the mistake.

The principal of the school was given all of this information by the physical education teacher. He contacted Martha's mother, who agreed to come to school as soon as her emergency room shift ended. Until then, Martha would be in the school's in-school suspension room. Martha was given some material to read about stealing, about making decisions, and about selecting friends.

The principal, a middle school counselor, the school's social worker, the physical education teacher, Martha's mother, and Martha met soon after the school day ended. Martha's mother made no excuses for Martha. Martha made no excuses for herself. The school's social worker had met with Martha during the afternoon and got her to open up about how this theft scheme had originated. They also talked about school overall and what Martha could do to improve her grades. The social worker talked to the principal and to the school counselor before the larger meeting. They explored some options and concluded that Martha needed to be punished and that Martha's middle school career needed a drastic correction.

The decision was to assign Martha to the in-school suspension room for two full days of school, to assign Martha a week of school service, which would include helping to clean the cafeteria after breakfast and after lunch, changing Martha's schedule so she would not be in physical education class, and requiring Martha to attend the school's after-school tutoring program on Tuesdays and Thursdays so she could complete homework, prepare for tests, get needed academic assistance, and complete a reading skills program. Martha would also apologize to the two students she had stolen from.

Martha's mother made some changes at home. Martha's cell phone was taken from her for the rest of the school year. Martha's computer privileges were reduced to using the computer at home only when her mother was home and only in the family room where her mother could see what Martha was doing. Martha finally told her mother about her new friends and that was not easy because she felt some type of loyalty to them even though they had been part of the whole sequence of events that got her in trouble. Martha's mother insisted that Martha have nothing to do with these new friends.

The days of in-school suspension were tedious for Martha. She did not like classes, but classes were better than in-school suspension. She had schoolwork to do, she had to meet with a school counselor, she had to meet with the school social worker, she had to clean the cafeteria, and she never saw any of her real friends, but she also did not see her new friends. In fact, she asked her school counselor to change her schedule so she would have no classes with those students, and the schedule change was made.

In a few weeks, something else started to change. Martha's grades, which had always been D's and C's, moved up to C's and B's. The Tuesday and Thursday after-school tutorial work was helping. Plus, the social worker and the school counselor each checked in with Martha weekly. They monitored her grades. They got updates from her teachers. They kept in touch with Martha's mother.

The supervisor of the in-school suspension program also sponsors the school's speech team. She noticed that Martha was very articulate. She asked Martha about coming to a meeting of the speech team on Wednesday after school. Martha was reluctant, but when told that pizza would be available, she got more interested. Martha's mother had decided that Martha's sister in elementary school should stay in the after-school program there on days that Martha had tutoring, so adding Wednesday worked fine for Martha to try Speech Club and for her sister to stay at the elementary school until Martha went over there and they walked home together.

Martha and Speech Club were a great match. Martha decided to specialize in something called impromptu presentations. This meant you were given a topic and almost instantly you made a two-minute presentation about it. Martha could talk about any subject. She had many ideas and opinions.

Martha was told that Speech Club participated in several speech contests. Students from various schools attended these contests, gave speeches, and were judged by high school teachers or college professors. Martha came in second place in her first speech contest. She continued to practice, improve, and compete. She eventually came in first place in a speech contest as a 7th grader. Martha and her speech coach began to set some high goals for her 8th grade year of speech contests. They also set goals for Martha's grades and Martha's behavior.

The in-school suspension supervisor and the school counselor talked one day about Martha. They asked themselves what could have been done to get Martha on the right path before she got in trouble for stealing. They were concerned that it took a stealing incident for all of the actions to be implemented that were making so many beneficial changes in Martha, in her grades, in her ambitions, in her new achievements, in her behavior, and in what she expected of herself.

They thought about how many other students in the school were similar to what Martha had been. How could they identify each of those students? How could they redirect each of those students? There had to be a way. They were determined to find a way or to make one.

The two school counselors, the social worker, the principal, the assistant principal, and the school's reading specialist met to create a plan. There were six people in this group. There were six core teaching teams in the school, two teams at each grade level. The six people in this group would each take a team and meet with the team once per week. Each week, the team would identify three students, one from each of the following groups: (1) at risk of failing this year, (2) passing grades or average grades, but can do much better, and (3) good grades but not challenged enough.

The teaching team and the person on the UP group (UP stands for Unlimited Potential and was suggested by the school's social worker) assigned to that team would meet with the three students to identify areas of improvement to work on and enhanced opportunities for new challenges. This would continue for ten weeks until each team had identified thirty students. Progress would be measured, monitored, and evaluated. Changes would be made as necessary. Parents and guardians of students involved in the UP process would be notified, updated, and asked to increase their involvement in what their child was doing at school, plus to reinforce the school effort with additional supportive actions at home.

UP would not be 100 percent successful, but it would make a difference in many lives. Some, perhaps most of the UP students, would improve their grades, improve their behavior, or grow with acceptance of and completion of new challenges. For the UP students who responded well to this new opportunity, middle school would be more right than it had been before and than it otherwise would have been. For the middle school educators who made this extra effort, a sense of achievement would be gained along with the personal peace of knowing that an extra effort was made to touch lives at a pivotal age for students when the return on the investment of time, work, attention, and concern can be maximized.

Does it take time to establish, to implement, and to maintain the UP program? Yes. Does dealing with underachieving students and disobedient students take time? Yes. Could the UP program or similar efforts shift some educator time from the "dealing with problems" category to the "preventing problems" and "creating results" categories? Yes. Could the UP program mean that students who are making A's, but are not fully challenged, could get the experiences they deserve and need? Yes. Does Unlimited Potential sound like a definition of or a synonym for middle school? Yes!

TREVOR—MAYBE HIGH SCHOOL WILL BE BETTER

Trevor Stevenson is a likable 8th grader. He never gets in serious trouble. He is a bit mischievous, but he is not harmful to anyone. His parents say he just acts silly sometimes, but that he behaves at home. His teachers say he should pay attention better, concentrate more, work harder, turn in work consistently, and speak only when called on, but that he is certainly not at risk of failing any classes. Trevor makes C grades, almost never a D or a B. Trevor is in the habit of making C's and he is satisfied with that. It could be worse, but it could be so much better.

In 6th grade, Trevor made C grades. In 7th grade, Trevor made C grades. Nothing has changed in 8th grade where Trevor continues to make C's.

Teachers have talked to Trevor. He is polite, but nothing changes. The principal of the school created a new type of Honor Roll for students who improved their grades. If you had a C average, calculated on a four-point scale as a 2.0 average, and the average increased on the next report card by 0.5 or more, you would be rewarded. Trevor's average never dropped below 2.0, but it never rose to 2.5 or above. Trevor was quite satisfied with C's.

Standardized testing usually showed that Trevor had the intellect to make better grades, but the work ethic or the willingness or just the attitude that making better grades matters were all elusive. It could be worse, but it could be so much better.

Eighth graders at Trevor's middle school take an interest inventory that is used by the middle school counselors and the high school counselors to help create class schedules for 9th graders. Trevor's interest is cars in particular and mechanical work in general. Trevor's plan is to learn how to repair cars. His father has taught him about basic car maintenance and upkeep and repair. Trevor would like to go to vocational now and study car repair, but to get in that program he has to be a high school sophomore.

Trevor will finish 8th grade with a C average. He will move to high school and probably make C's as a ninth grader. During ninth grade he will apply for the car repair program in the school district's vocational school. It is likely that he will make A and B grades in all of his vocational school classes. He would make A and B grades now in vocational school classes if 8th graders were allowed to take those classes or to take 8th grade level introductory classes that lead to the high school vocational program.

Why must all 8th graders take the same classes? Why must vocational programs be available only to high school students? Why not have vocational skill programs for middle school students and embed the academic subjects they also need within the overall vocational curriculum?

Why not improve the reading skills of an 8th grader, who is someday going to be a master automobile craftsman, by having that student read, read more, and keep reading about cars? The student could study the history of cars, study the science of cars, read about the lives of people who invented cars, do the math of cars, and do the critical thinking that car repair requires.

Why deny great achievement with cars and the associated great academic learning that can connect with cars to an 8th grader who otherwise will make C's in the regular 8th grade classes? Why keep Trevor in an average experience making average grades when he could excel in another program that he would commit to fully today, but that will not commit at all to Trevor today?

Why take the risk that things will be better in high school for Trevor? Trevor is ready to commit now. Why wait and hope that he has the same willingness to commit two years from now? Why not get bold, get creative, get innovative, and make middle school right for Trevor now?

Middle school students are real people living real lives right now. Because of their youth, they may not fully realize how vital it is to maximize the educational results of their middle school years. Yet also because of their youth they do seek to maximize the excitement, the discovery, the understanding, and the experiences of the middle school years. The power for the good of these middle school years is a vital resource that middle school educators can maximize through honorable, conscientious, relentless effort for Ellen, Martha, Trevor, and every other middle school student. There simply is no substitute for getting education right in middle school for Ellen, Martha, Trevor, and every other middle school student.

Chapter Ten

Middle School Stories

"When do we get to do another project?" asked the 7th grader very sincerely and with obvious eagerness. The teacher had no answer. The school year would be over in less than two weeks. The teacher had not planned for or scheduled another project.

Yet the good question deserved an equally good answer. The teacher thought quickly and a little desperately. Finally, there was an answer. "Soon. What did you have in mind?" The teacher hoped that the student could help answer the question.

"I'm really interested in roller coasters," the student explained. "I'd like to do some work on roller coasters." The teacher was thrilled when he heard the words "I'd like to do some work" because it was unusual for students to request more work.

The teacher then asked every 7th grader in the critical thinking class what topic they would like to work on. "Fashion," "baseball," "money," "television," and "cheerleading" were some of the answers. The teacher promised to create the details of the next project in time for class the next day.

The project was for each student to create a magazine about the topic of their choice, knowing that each topic had to meet the perennial requirements of everything in this class: G-rated, legal, and ethical. The students were told the requirements: front cover with an illustration, the magazine name, and information about this issue; advertisements on the inside front cover, inside back cover, and on the back cover; a table of contents; at least five articles, two of which must be the student's original writing; letters to the editor; a mail-in card to subscribe to the magazine; and a preview of the next issue.

The magazines were masterpieces. The work was superior. The students learned much about their topics and about research. They had to think, to create, to work. Everyone turned in the project on time, done completely, and done correctly. All magazines were excellent and all magazines were different.

The project mattered to the students. The project was not preparation for high school. The project was maximizing this moment, right now, right here. The project was middle school–friendly and middle school–meaningful and middle school–real. Maximizing the vital middle school years involves maximizing the moments within those middle school years. The unexpected-yet-glorious question from that intellectually active 7th grader presented a moment to maximize.

Right here, right now. Middle school matters right here, right now. Middle school is its own unique time, place, and experience. Middle school is not elementary school extended or high school anticipated. Middle school is its own time, place, and experience, which present vital years that long to be maximized for uniquely developing students who need the maximum opportunity for academic achievement and for personal growth.

In the first day of economics class, an elective for 8th graders, the teacher began class by asking this compelling question: "How many of you would like to become millionaires? Raise your hand if your answer is yes." Each student responded with an enthusiastic yes.

The students and their teacher then did Individual Retirement Account (IRA) math to see how saving money and letting it grow for decades could result in millionaire status and, perhaps, in higher status than that. The students were convinced that an IRA was a good idea, but with a payoff in fifty years, there was an interest in finding some results that occur faster.

The teacher created Individual Reward Accounts. Students earned points for their classroom IRA with great questions or answers in class, with very good grades on tests or projects, and with superior conduct in class. As the IRA accounts grew, the students wondered how those points would be used. The teacher created a store that had a wide variety of snacks and school supplies. Each item in the store had a price that was expressed in terms of IRA points.

On the day in class when the store was having its grand opening, some students quickly shopped. These students sought the best selection. Other students watched the early shoppers but spent no IRA points. They had been taught the importance of saving, so they were not spending. A few students commented that the prices were too high. Price reductions followed and a few students responded to that, but most of the students who did not spend points at first were still not spending points even with the lower prices.

After class, two very confident and very creative 8th graders approached the teacher and announced "We're going to compete with you tomorrow. We're going to create our own store." The two entrepreneurs were excited. The teacher was thrilled. The classroom marketplace would be extra vibrant tomorrow and learning about economics would reach new levels.

The student store attracted many shoppers who were impressed with the new selections. The entrepreneurs knew what snacks other 8th graders liked best. The teacher had restocked his supplies according to what sold well on the Grand Opening day. Customers moved between the stores in search of better deals and in hopes of reduced prices. Economic activity increased as did real understanding of economics.

The two entrepreneurs collected many IRA points that students spent at their store. These points could be spent at the teacher's store. To reward the two 8th grade business innovators, the IRA points they collected through sales were doubled, so they were able to buy much of what the teacher's store still had in stock.

That bonus pleased those two students, but their greater joy came from successfully competing in the classroom marketplace. The teacher was equally joyous as he acknowledged the effort, the creativity, and the success of the two entrepreneurs. The teacher was also pleased that the students felt so comfortable that they could compete with the teacher's store. They were not afraid that the teacher would resent the competition; rather, they knew that in this classroom their input was highly valued and sincerely sought.

The competing store was a great tribute to the creativity, energy, spirit, spunk, and gumption that is within middle school students. Those characteristics were quite free in this classroom to be applied, nurtured, and developed. The teacher was in charge, yet the students were active partners in their own education. Middle school was not something imposed on these economics students. Middle school was experienced with an interactive, creative, productive, practical way by these students.

No new government regulation, policy, or law was needed. No funding source was needed. A classroom experience that intrigued students, inspired students, involved students, and that applied the inherent curiosity, energy, and competitiveness of students brought about significant results. Middle school can do that.

The 7th graders in citizenship class were studying the ongoing presidential primary elections and the overall process of nominating candidates. The students were especially curious about several well-known, highly respected, potentially strong contenders who had decided not to seek their political party's nomination for president. The students wondered why a person who had the credentials, who was encouraged by prominent people to run, and who did well in public opinion polls would not become a candidate.

The students took the names of these non-candidates and their biographies to merge all of that into a fictional candidate whose name and career were hybrids of the non-candidates. The students made signs, made speeches, and wrote a campaign song. The fictional candidate became the ideal choice of many of these students.

Then the fictional candidate was matched up in competition with the actual announced candidates. Upon closer scrutiny the students began to notice achievements of and ideas of the announced candidates that were as good as or better than those of the non-candidates or the fictional candidate. They learned some practical insights about the ideals of politics and the reality of politics. They also concluded that their campaign materials were designed better than those that real candidates were actually using.

The energy, the excitement, and the learning in the classroom were at very high and very intellectual levels when the students did enough research to make a candidate and to present that candidate's ideas, resume, materials, song, and slogan. The activity was designed to cause learning right here, right now in this 7th grade citizenship classroom with, of, by, and for these 7th graders. It worked for many reasons that the reader can pause to consider.

Another group of 7th grade citizenship students were interested in classroom activities that borrowed methods from television game shows or from traditional board games. The teacher sometimes asked the students, one student at a time, short answer questions such as "Who is the president of the United States?" "Who is the Supreme Court chief justice?" "How many U.S. senators are there total?" "How many members are in the U.S. House of Representatives total?" and "How old does the constitution say a U. S. president must be?"

As the school year progressed and more topics were studied, the list of specific, objective questions increased. When the list got to one hundred questions, the students were eager to see if they could answer all of the questions correctly. To add some drama, it was agreed that there would be a four-minute limit. The teacher would go from one student to the next student in turn and would ask the first question. If the first student correctly answered the first question, the teacher then asked the second student to answer the next question. If the answer was incorrect, the third student would answer the same question.

The first effort resulted in thirty-seven correct answers in four minutes. The students were certain that they could improve. The teacher agreed to try the "four-minute drill" each day until the goal of one hundred correct answers was reached. In only a few days the students were beyond one hundred answers in four minutes, so the teacher began the list over again as time allowed.

There was a day when everything went perfectly. Attention was 100 percent. Concentration was 100 percent. Every answer was swift and accurate. All of the one hundred questions were answered correctly again. Time remained, so the teacher began asking the questions a third time. When the four minutes ended everyone knew that a record had been set. When the teacher said, "Congratulations, you answered 217 questions," the classroom was filled with cheers and smiles. Athletic events do not get louder celebrations.

What aspects of the four-minute drill made that activity work so well with 7th graders? What aspects of that activity apply some of the unique characteristics of middle school students? What traits of middle school students are put to very productive use in the four-minute drill? What modifications, if any, would be necessary to make the four-minute drill work well for 6th graders or for 8th graders? What are the benefits for students and for a teacher of the four-minute drill?

THE FRUSTRATED, EXHAUSTED, DETERMINED MIDDLE SCHOOL TEACHER

When will this school year end? I'm not sure I can make it until the end of the year. How many sick days do I have? When would it be conspicuous if I started being absent fairly often? It's only February. We have March, April, and May yet to go. I really am not sure I can make it through this school year.

The year began fairly well except for those changes in the testing system we were told about in August. We have had so many questions about these new tests, but nobody has clear answers. So in May our students will take new tests that the state government requires and that the national government says states have to do. Well, since nobody can really tell us much about these new tests, how am I supposed to prepare my students?

Then there are all of those walk-throughs about once a week, at least it feels that way, when somebody from the higher-up levels in the school district comes into my classroom for about five minutes. They have some checklist they use to evaluate how I am doing my job. I think I do my job well, but those checklists always say there are things I have to improve. I'd like to see a walk-through at my house on Saturday or Sunday when I'm grading papers, but I doubt the walk-through people work on weekends.

We're told to build relationships with the students. I do that. I get to know them, their interests, their strengths, their weaknesses, their goals. I don't learn all of that with a walk-through and a checklist. So why not get to know me and what my job is like? The people in those big jobs tell me to get to know the students. Well, lead by example. Visit my class and stay for an hour and then talk to me about what you observed. There's a lot we could discuss, but when you walk in, walk through, and walk out, it looks like you prefer to avoid any serious interaction. Why are you like that?

The teachers have been told that every student must have a writing assignment each week in every class. This is to be at least one page long. It has to be graded thoroughly for writing accuracy and for the content of the ideas and it has to be returned, graded, with comments to the students within three days.

I was already putting sixty-five hours each week into this job. Am I supposed to increase that to seventy-five hours each week, or am I supposed to eliminate ten hours of other work? If I eliminate anything then my students miss out on something they need. We're asked to do more every year. I think I've reached my limit.

Our school board just passed a policy that says no student will fail 6th, 7th, or 8th grade. They are telling every middle school to make all necessary changes and take every action needed so any student with an F grade or more than one F grade on the first report card will get remedial instruction to make up what was not done right.

We are supposed to find a way to get every failing student caught up on what they did not learn, make sure they learn the new stuff we are working on, and keep everyone else at a passing grade or higher. They gave us zero suggestions on how to get all of that done. They said each school should do what works at that school. I think what works is being trusted to do my job and being left alone to get that job done.

The school board also said that each middle school student is to get thirty minutes of physical activity daily. The physical education classes use the gym all day, so nobody else can go there. Are we really supposed to do physical exercise activity in our classrooms? Where do we get those thirty minutes? Will the school day become longer? Do I reduce instruction time in each class by four or five minutes so we can do calisthenics? Do the people who make these decisions ever ask for ideas from the people who will actually carry out the decision?

I'll do everything I am told to do. I'll find a way. I have to. I've been a middle school teacher for twelve years. I can't change careers at this point. I just wish that teachers could be left alone to do our job, to teach. All of this other stuff that gets added on really makes it worse for students.

Middle school students need teachers who have the time and the talent to really work with this age group. I have the talent and the experience and the knowledge. I think my time with the students in my classroom needs to be for me to teach them so they learn everything in the curriculum for my class. I can do that but I have to be protected from all this other stuff that interferes.

The teacher above is frustrated and exhausted yet determined. Which of her concerns and complaints are most valid? How could those concerns and complaints most effectively be addressed? Which of her concerns and complaints are not as valid or are not valid at all? What action or acknowledgment toward those concerns and complaints should be taken, if any? What does she offer that should be affirmed, valued, appreciated, and noticed? What guidance, advice, or professional development could be helpful for her?

THE INTRIGUED, ENERGETIC, OPTIMISTIC, IDEALISTIC MIDDLE SCHOOL TEACHER

I went to a middle school teacher's conference during the summer and every guest speaker kept saying that the teacher is now a facilitator. What a terrible idea. I disagreed with every speaker at that conference. I hope they were not paid to speak, but I'm afraid they were. I did not go to college or graduate school to earn degrees in and certification for facilitation. I went to college and to graduate school to learn all about math and all about how to teach math. I'm a teacher. My job is to make sure that students learn. My job is not to just guide the students along as they figure out math on their own. I'm supposed to show them how to figure it out. I show them how to do what they don't yet know how to do.

I work hard with my students. I arrive early and if they need extra help they come to my classroom before the first class on any day. They can come to my classroom after school for help. If it takes extra time, I'll give them the extra time.

My classroom is lively. If we ever do a math worksheet it is a worksheet I created. If we do word problems, I write the problems and I use names of my students in the problems. I even use situations the students can relate to. My students last year were crazy about some new fashion and some sports team and a new movie, so we did really difficult math word problems on those topics. They loved it and they learned the math.

I also coach the girl's basketball team and I sponsor our Community Service Volunteer Club. I think it's good to work with the students on things outside of the classroom. It shows me more about them. I can use that knowledge in my teaching.

This is my fifth year of teaching. I'm a mentor to a first-year teacher. I really hope he has a great first year. I try to encourage him with his 6th grade math classes. He says the job is a lot harder than he expected it to be, so I need to help him learn about how to manage all the stuff we have to do.

The principal asked me to serve on a curriculum revision committee for our school. I am glad to do that. I'm also the team leader on our 8th grade teaching team this year. The team leader I worked with the last four years was counting the days until retirement, so our team needs some new energy and I can do that.

My friends and my family tell me I work too hard, but I disagree. I'm at school all the time, I'll admit that, or I'm at home working on school, but that's what I do. The harder I work, the better my students do, so I keep working hard. This work really fascinates me. These students can learn so much. I intend to see them do their best, so I have to do my best. I'm young and optimistic. I'm doing the work I always intended to do. I hope that nothing gets in my way.

What could get in the way of this idealistic, optimistic, intrigued middle school teacher? Is he accepting too many duties? Is he going to burn out in a few years? Is he thriving and does he need to be allowed to keep doing everything he is involved with because it is good for his students and good for him? What advice and guidance could be helpful for this teacher? Could he become a good middle school counselor or middle school administrator? Or should he stay in the classroom where he currently is getting such good results?

The point has been made that middle school students are real people living real lives right now. That aphorism confirms the importance of making the middle school experience as unique, dynamic, and energetic as the middle school students themselves are while also directing them and guiding them.

Middle school educators and staff also are real people living real lives right now. The middle school experience for students is shaped more by the educators and staff at the middle school than by any other people. These educators and staff members should be listened to whenever possible and led whenever necessary. Encouragement, support, and appreciation can be provided to those educators and staff members in many ways, large and small, that make significant differences in the attitude and the achievements of those adults. Taking good care of middle school educators and staff members makes it possible for them to take good care of middle school students.

The survey participants were given an opportunity to share additional thoughts that they found to be important. Some of those insights follow.

- "Students can be on top of the world one minute, at the bottom of the well the next. Enjoy the ride!"
- "This is the most challenging time for students in terms of physical, emotional, psychological changes."
- "Students will perform for you if they respect you, not because they fear you. However, people often confuse developing a mentoring relationship and being a student's 'friend.' They don't need adults in their life to be their friends. They need them to guide them along the right path, which means you may make them mad at times."
- "Middle school educators need to have lots of patience, lots of imagination, and a 'sack' full of surprises."
- "Involve yourself in the school community and in activities. Developing relationships and meeting student needs is not a 9:00 to 5:00 job."
- "A person really needs to be patient, understanding, and real for middle schoolers to gain respect for them."
- "It can be a rewarding time of tremendous growth and an awkward time of discovery."
- "Middle school students want to please, especially those who set high standards and believe in their abilities."
- "You have to love it to be a part of it."

One very important thought that emerges from those ideas is that working at a middle school is quite different than working at either an elementary school or a high school. Some educators would never consider middle school work. Some educators would consider only middle school work. Know yourself and know which level of education work is the best match for you so you will be the right person for that level.

PLEASE NOTICE ME EVEN WHEN I ASK YOU TO LEAVE ME ALONE: A MIDDLE SCHOOL STUDENT'S REQUEST

I am a 6th grader in your English class. I'm kind of scared about being in this big middle school. I would never ask, but it sure would help if you show me around this place and then be sure I can open my locker. Well, first be sure I can find my locker.

I am a 7th grader in your math class. I hate math. I never do good work in math. Everyone tells me I have to do better. Please make me understand math. Math never makes sense to me. Math teachers talk too fast. We have too many math problems to do. I can't do one problem, so why do math teachers give me twenty problems to do? I would be embarrassed to ask a question in class so please notice when I should ask a question and come help me.

I am an 8th grader in your art class. I actually like art, but not school art. I like different types of art. My friend works at a t-shirt place and he designs art for shirts. Why can't we do that in art class?

I'm a 7th grader who is new to this school. I miss my old school a lot. Can you do anything to make this place feel like my old school?

I'm a 6th grader, but I can do 7th grade work. Please don't make me sit through a year of dumb stuff I already know. Let me learn something new.

I'm an 8th grader and I skip school pretty often. School is dumb. I failed 6th grade. I intend to drop out when I'm old enough.

I'm a 7th grader and I had the worst summer ever. My parents got divorced. It's awful. I really don't care much about school right now. Maybe you could take it easy on me.

I'm an 8th grader and I tried out for the basketball team the past two years. I never made the team, but I've really grown a lot in the past year. I think I'm the tallest student in my class. I might try out, but I don't want to get told no again. What do you think I should do?

I'm in 7th grade, but there's this 8th grade boy who likes me. I don't think I like him. He's cute and stuff, but there's another boy I like better, but he ignores me. It's all so stupid, but I do like that one boy. How can I get him to notice me?

I'm in the 7th grade. I never get in trouble. I make good grades. I have a lot of friends. They make good grades and stay out of trouble. From what I can tell the only students here who get noticed are the ones who get in trouble all the time or the ones who play sports. That's not fair.

I'm in the 8th grade. I'm a pretty good student. I don't cause problems. I just wish we had stuff at school that I care about. You know, I like airplanes. I think I want to be in the Air Force and be a pilot. We don't have anything here about that. Why not?

I'm in the 8th grade and I'm a criminal. That's just how it is. I got caught stealing stuff from a store. I got arrested and put on probation. Then I stole again. I got arrested and put in juvenile jail. So do you think your school has anything for me? Jail was no big deal so what can you do to me?

I'm in the 6th grade. I'm lost here. Please help me figure this place out.

I'm in the 6th grade. I love this school. The library is fantastic. I want to read every book here. This place is so cool.

The most accurate, honest, liberating answer to the question "How do we improve schools?" is that there is not one answer to that question. There are endless answers to that question because the human variables are endless.

There is hope. We know what works. There are great educators at elementary schools, middle schools, and high schools. Ask them. They will be glad to tell you what works. Observe them. They will be glad to show you what works.

There are exemplary middle schools and there are exemplary middle school educators. These schools and these educators know how to guide 6th, 7th, and 8th graders through the difficulties and the opportunities of the middle school maze. Ask them what they know. They are not keeping secrets. Observe them. Their talents are on display daily.

Middle school students are real people living real lives right now. Middle school educators are real people doing really vital work right now. Maximizing the productivity of, the meaningful activities in, and the guiding experiences of middle school is what the students need and is what brings the greatest reward to the educators. Maximize the middle school years because they are some of the most maximize-able years of all.

About the Author

Keen J. Babbage has twenty-eight years of experience as a teacher and administrator in middle school, high school, college, and graduate school. He is the author of the following books:

Reform Doesn't Work: Grassroots Efforts Can Provide Answers to School Improvement (2012)

The Dream and Reality of Teaching: Becoming the Best Teacher Students Ever Had (2011)

The Extreme Principle: What Matters Most, What Works Best (2010)

Extreme Writing: Discovering the Writer in Every Student (2010)

What Only Teachers Know about Education: The Reality of the Classroom (2008)

Extreme Economics: The Need for Personal Finance in the School Curriculum (2007, 2009)

Results-Driven Teaching: Teach So Well That Every Student Learns (2006)

Extreme Students: Challenging All Students and Energizing Learning (2005)

Extreme Learning (2004)

Extreme Teaching (2002)

High-Impact Teaching: Overcoming Student Apathy (1998)

Meetings for School-Based Decision Making (1997)

911: The School Administrator's Guide to Crisis Management (1996)